AnF

155.937

KU-606-819

WITHDRAWN FROM STOCK
DUBLIN CITY PUBLIC LIBRARIES

Leabharlann na Cabraí
Cabra Library
01-2228317

'An important book about the ways fiction can provide escape and hope and meaning in the face of unbearable pain. The ways it can teach and guide and contain, illuminating the darkness. A book about the marvel and wonder of children, and our terror for them, when things change in ways we can neither predict nor control. A book about love and story, and why one is essential to the other. Deeply moving, compelling and thought-provoking, *Bedtime Story* explores the reasons why we write for children, the mystery we are trying to get to the heart of, the tools we are trying to give to our young people to survive. A book about the ways we can triumph over loss and grief, with the stories that we write, the worlds we draw. Deeply engrossing and honest, human, full of love and tenderness, with moments of sparkling humour in the struggle. I loved everything about *Bedtime Story*. I loved particularly what it taught me about authors who write for children, the ways that writing and reading provides compensation, balancing the scales between loss and love.'
—Sofie Laguna, author of *The Eye of the Sheep* and *Too Loud Lily*

'This book is a miracle of light and meaning-making from one of our finest writers. Venturing inward with extraordinary grace, Hooper explores—and extends—the long literary line surging with our deepest inherited wisdom about how to embrace our finite lives. The result is nothing less than the hero's journey we have been collectively starving for. Telling you this is like trying to describe the sun; it is a book so powerful and beautiful—so utterly its own—that it can only be experienced directly.' —Sarah Krasnostein, author of *The Trauma Cleaner* and *The Believer*

'Chloe Hooper has a formidable talent to take complex stories and ideas and truths, and to distil them into a language of direct and powerful beauty. This is a story of grief and of patience, of hope and acceptance. It is also a reminder of the solace that books give us, and of how the imaginary worlds we dive into as children remain with us for all our lives, of how they guide us into adulthood and maturity. There is a quiet courage and strength in this book. It is both gentle and uncompromising, a love letter to family and to literature that is bracingly unsentimental. I was profoundly moved, and profoundly grateful.' —Christos Tsiolkas, author of *The Slap* and *Damascus*

# Bedtime Story

Leabharlanna Chathair Bhaile Átha Cliath
Dublin City Libraries

# Chloe Hooper

# Bedtime Story

Illustrated by Anna Walker

## SCRIBNER

LONDON NEW YORK SYDNEY TORONTO NEW DELHI

First published in Australia by Scribner, an imprint of Simon & Schuster Australia, 2022

First published in Great Britain by Scribner, an imprint of Simon & Schuster UK Ltd, 2022

Copyright © Chloe Hooper, 2022

The right of Chloe Hooper to be identified as the author
of this work has been asserted in accordance with the
Copyright, Designs and Patents Act, 1988.

SCRIBNER and design are registered trademarks of The Gale Group, Inc.,
used under licence by Simon & Schuster Inc.

1 3 5 7 9 10 8 6 4 2

Simon & Schuster UK Ltd
1st Floor
222 Gray's Inn Road
London WC1X 8HB

www.simonandschuster.co.uk
www.simonandschuster.com.au
www.simonandschuster.co.in

Simon & Schuster Australia, Sydney
Simon & Schuster India, New Delhi

The author and publishers have made all reasonable efforts to contact
copyright-holders for permission, and apologise for any omissions or errors in
the form of credits given. Corrections may be made to future printings.

A CIP catalogue record for this book is available from the British Library

Hardback ISBN: 978-1-3985-1058-6
eBook ISBN: 978-1-3985-1059-3

Interior design by Allison Colpoys
Internal illustrations by Anna Walker

Printed and bound by Bell & Bain

MIX
Paper from
responsible sources
FSC
www.fsc.org
FSC® C007785

For T & G

# One

Every night when the light's switched off, familiar objects in your room mutate. What daylight tames, the dark untames. Bookshelves, reading lamp, a dressing gown draped on the door, all gather a silent force. The stillness feels alive, as if each thing is deciding how to behave.

At first, there's a thrill to this sudden chaos. You're not yet listening to the in-and-out of your own breathing, not yet decoding the noises in and outside the house. The shimmer of the dark makes climbing into bed feel less like surrendering. You've used all your wiles to put off this moment, and yet it turns out your limbs are heavy and the sheets are cool.

You wait while we draw the curtains against the night (or any dawn waking). You wait as we straighten you and your brother's bedclothes; already he can't stop his eyelids from closing. You keep waiting and we reshelve the picture books. On these books' pages life is reduced to its essential elements. The sun is a yellow ball in the sky. The road a black ribbon leading to green. The woods are reliably timbered, and within them a monster is a monster; no need to factor in *his* childhood. The stories are soothing because the turnings of the plot are so well-worn, their surprises practised. Each night people are sad then happy. They get lost and found, and return to their houses that have a front door between two windows.

It doesn't occur to your father or me to tell you what is really happening here inside this house. Why the force between objects is charged differently for us too. We don't want to let dread through the bedroom door. And we don't want anything about these nights to change. All the most mundane tasks—toothbrushes cajoled into mouths, limbs into pyjamas—are suddenly revealed as precious, and if we diverge from the nightly routine in any way, everything could break apart.

There's a couch set against the wall between you and your brother's beds. Your father sits there in the glow of a planet-earth nightlight. If you turn you can see his profile. Glasses on a still boyish nose, but a forehead lined deeply; sometimes there's the win, even in the dark, of breaking through the thicket of his thoughts to make him smile.

Your father—Don, as you call him—is older than your friends' fathers, you know this. (I was born in the 'olden days', as you put it, but he in the 'olden, olden days'.) One of the advantages of his age is that he knows more stories, and you prefer him to put you to bed because then the picture books are only the prelude. When he's finished reading, he makes up something just for you. Both of us are writers although the original bedtime tales are his domain.

You lie in the fresh anarchy of the dark, waiting for his voice with an electric attention. But standing by the light switch, I know I need to find a way to talk with you about the shadows.

A child's fear of the dark may not even be about the dark. The heightened sense that something hideous waits in the dimness may be born when children start to learn there are mysteries they can't fathom. A veil is drawn back slightly: the child intuits the scale of things which cannot be controlled.

The beginning of these hours alone in a closed and unlit, or barely lit, space becomes perilous. Even a heartbeat could give someone away. In the 1920s the developmental psychologist Jean Piaget recorded rituals that children devise to keep themselves safe, observing: 'A boy who lived in a somewhat lonely house' believed 'if he could succeed in drawing the curtains very quickly the robbers would not come'. Other such 'rites to ward off danger' included 'hiding under the bedclothes, turning the back to the door, drawing the blanket up to exactly the chin, etc … Another felt protected if on getting into bed, the clothes were completely tucked in all around so that she could slip in without anywhere unmaking the bed. If by chance she found the clothes not tucked in, or, that they had come unmade as she got in, she felt herself threatened by danger.'

Perversely, adults set about peopling, or rather monstering, the dark for kids—to instruct or entertain or to control them.

The bottomless, complicated evil of the world we codify into witches and ogres, into the grim figures that your six-year-old brain now imagines reaching out and grabbing you. Yet hob-goblins and bugaboos are dangers you'll never actually need to confront.

Cancer is the bogeyman for adults. Later, in the pandemic, people will come to fear droplets of others' spit and snot—stuff kids trade in unblinkingly—but that contagion works by a series of links, a chain of contamination stretching back to an ani-mal and a human's ill-fated encounter; the terror in this case is outside, potentially everywhere. Cancer comes from within and provokes a different form of panic. A person walks down the street, leading a regular life, and suddenly *they* are the one. Any part of a body is vulnerable. It can find a home in an eye, throat, ovary, bladder, testicle, brain, breast—one's most hidden or prized part—then spread.

Before our recent visit to the hospital, your father's mood darkened: how seamlessly in these moments the surrealism kicks in. We'd initially been told his leukaemia was not a dangerous one. The haematologist, a droll woman, swollen with pregnancy, assured us that fortunes had been spent to make certain blood cancers, common in older white men, non-fatal. But she ordered extra tests anyway, and we had walked to her office down a seem-ingly endless hallway to hear the results. In a luminous white room, she showed us scans revealing enlarged lymph nodes throughout your father's body. The cancer levels in his blood had risen in just a fortnight. The haematologist had never seen this particular strain of leukaemia, she told us, and was seeking her colleagues' advice.

Don had the taciturn manner of an old farmer on a visit to the city. He was dressed like one too: a navy jumper over a shirt with a collar never sitting right. 'How long do I have?'

'You want this conversation?' she checked briskly.

If it was one form of leukaemia, five years. If it was a 'feral' form—and her manner hinted that this was her suspicion—there would be far less time. To discover his fate, Don needed to sign a form permitting further tests, on his bone marrow. These results would take a month.

Four whole weeks. Twenty-eight days before he's to return to the neat purgatory of the waiting room so as to wait some more—and in the meantime I have to start to educate you about the real dark.

Amidst your father's strife, this is surely one task I can handle. But how do I explain something that adults find near impossible to fathom? Only clichés rear up at me. Should I tell you not to be scared? Why would you not be? Should I say that sickness and death are natural? But so are many terrifying things.

I begin to imagine a book that I will find and read to you. It will be written simply, clearly; gently levering open a crushing conversation, with each illustration capturing some essential poetry. Perhaps these images are initially black and white, before colour rushes in towards the end, with golden, hope-flecked fireworks blooming on the last page. A finale signalling that this will one day be bearable, there will be grace! And meanwhile, the text won't have said too much or too little, providing us, wonderfully, with a map of how to survive. If I squint, I can almost see it, this perfect children's picture book of death …

That's what I want. Only that.

Basically, I'm telling *myself* a children's story: in a crisis we revert to the safety of the plot that ends happily.

As slowly the month of evenings starts to pass, I cast my eye, yet again over your shelves, searching for anything I might have forgotten, any book that will help us practise the unhappy ending.

Traditional children's literature is soaked in death. You have a beautifully illustrated edition of *Aesop's Fables*, every story a compact nature documentary; a fox kills, say, a bird to demonstrate a moral. You have a book of Greek myths that I found abandoned on the street in which family members kill each other; and of course, the fairytales, seemingly more humble affairs, where death has already visited. All may end well, but the tales are populated by orphans and widowers and infanticidal stepmothers.

Fairytales are thrillers for children. Over and over we've read them for the heart-quickening suspense. Will Hansel be eaten?

Will Jack
break his neck
climbing down the
beanstalk? Will Rapunzel,
escaping the tower? Will the wolf blow
down all the houses? (You covet our neighbours' brick homes
because of the pigs' travails.) Will the woodcutter arrive in time?

How long will Don survive?

I ask your father to record the stories he tells you. Neither of us needs to say why.

While your brother, Gabriel, is asleep amidst his zoo of soft animals, you lie still. This is your favourite way for the dark to be subdued. Your father's voice has mellow and gruff notes, making the sentences stretch and break, cracking the night open. The bed is a kind of boat then, and you are sailing …

… You're on holiday with your brother and your best friend, and you've seen a sign: 'Diving Tours'. Rustling up the money, the three of you climb aboard an old clinker. Out on the water it's a clear blue day, but it soon becomes apparent that the crew of one is incompetent. When a shark circles the boat, the skipper is sleeping off a hangover. Your companions are down on the ocean floor. Thinking quickly, you grind up some sleeping tablets you've found in the boat's medicine cabinet. You stuff this into sandwiches packed by the tour company for lunch, and throw them to the shark. *Zzzzzzzzz!* The divers are saved!

In Don's tale you are strong and clever and brave. And you accept that the adults around you barely know what they are doing.

Your father remains within arm's reach—all five feet nine inches of his stiff-necked, sun-reddened, impatient, funny, tender self—and in the globe-lit dark, he is bringing you into being word by word.

Storytellers offer more than just their voice; they are a companion on the adventure—and nothing can happen to the teller mid-tale. If Don keeps the narrative going, he's protected for another night. But 1001 of them will not be enough. They add up to only two and three-quarter years, and we need more time.

In children's stories, people exist in another element. If there's darkness, it serves to highlight the glint of the miraculous, animals turning and opening their mouths to offer priceless advice … In the past eighteen months, you've asked Don whether a favourite television show featuring a squad of cats and dogs is real. He asked if you'd seen any animals driving down our street recently. You considered this, looking unconvinced. Just because you hadn't seen such a spectacle didn't mean it wasn't possible. For young children, there's barely a division between the real and the imagined anyway. Being a fantasist holds no shame.

You believe in magic and when he's in your room telling you a bedtime story, he's allowed to think magically too. So, what can a string of words actually do? The idea of language being enchanted is an ancient one, but can a story save a person? Can the right one pull us back to life? Certainly, a book can save a slice of life, as anyone who rereads knows. Years later, a sentence will return a person to the very room they first found it in. Your father's stories transport the two of you somewhere else. Somewhere he can try to ward off what's to come. You are keeping the storyteller safe. He is holding the dark at bay for you, as are you for him.

# Two

'Will I ever die?'

You've asked the question before, but this time the tone is defiant, a dare. Do I have the audacity to suggest that *you*, a hug-averse spider expert with shining skin and a balletic punt kick, could ever face extinction?

The answer is absurd.

Our kitchen table, covered by Mexican oilcloth, the pattern repeating fistfuls of bright flowers, is nevertheless perfect for our own *Día de Muertos*. You have risen from your chair to sit *on* the tabletop. You're the king of the castle, but also with missing front teeth, a young Count Dracula, and you stretch insouciantly and reel off all the people we know, asking for confirmation of their mortality. Then, eyes fixed on mine, you come closer. It gets personal. Yes, *I* will die, I tell you. Your little brother, his chubby face bearded with dinner, will also die. And your father? There is a new tension to this conversation, and you are listening to me with a peculiar vigilance.

'Yes,' I admit, 'your father will die too.'

A few days have passed since that last visit with the haematologist.

On our way home from the appointment, Don and I stopped to have lunch. It was true autumn. Leaves fell from the plane trees outside the restaurant window, scattering down an empty street. Metaphoric weather, synching up like in a bad movie, while Don sat, his expression almost wry. Everyone who has small children feels tired, he'd thought it was just that. As I wept, the waitress placed a wineglass and then a plate under my bowed head as if nothing were amiss.

At home, we've tried to behave in a similar fashion: each night, your father has stood at the kitchen bench chopping vegetables into neat piles, preparing dinner. The set is the same, but the surfaces are unstable.

He seems chastened—is that what gives us away? Usually, his mind is wound pinwheel tight with sparks of wit and pique, a dazzling variety of furies spinning round him. Now he's strangely placid, and I'm pretending the sky won't fall in. Bad actors, we sit at the table next to you and Gabriel, both of you propped up with cushions.

Gabriel pivots between an expression of knowingness and deep oblivion. Right now, I prefer the latter. (Through the day, it's a solace to find him trying to start his toy fire truck with my car keys, or feeding his slice of apple to a stuffed rabbit. He's safe in another, perhaps richer world.) Tilting his silky head, he spoons away his meal while Don and I brace ourselves for your routine interrogation.

The questions, your questions: 'Do you prefer sunrises or sunsets?'; 'What was the first thing on earth?'; 'What's the most poisonous spider in the world?'; 'Do postmen open and read the letters they deliver?'; 'Is it true to say somewhere in the world, someone's home is on fire?' and, if not, 'Could a bag of dynamite blow up a house?'

'It depends how big the bag of dynamite is,' your father answers.

'The largest size.'

'Yes, it could.'

'Two houses?'

'Probably.'

'Three?'

'You might need a bag and a half,' he advises.

Each dinner turns into a symposium on, say, the different ways a household can implode, and I'm reminded I only half listened at school in classes that didn't interest me. I want—no, I need—your father around to answer your questions. I want him to have the pleasure of hearing them, and you his answers: the natural luxury of this dynamic. Don's ability to retain facts, sometimes so irritating, is, in the foggy countdown to bedtime, also invaluable. Don't ask me which planet is bigger, or colder, or furthest away. I've no idea, especially now. The earth apparently spins on its axis every twenty-four hours, and tomorrow I'll mark off this day. I'm going to do it a total of twenty-eight times. Using up a month of precious nights. Waiting, when we don't know what we're waiting for.

After dinner, there's a last stand. All the frustrations of living under adult rule come out in a nightly revolt. You throw your underpants onto the ceiling fan and retrieve them by turning it on high. You encourage your brother to dance on his bed, naked and holding a torch. We wave the bedtime story as a lion tamer wields a chair.

———

I decide to go back to the beginning. For all of human history—save a few generations in a few rich places—children have lived close up with death. What have adults told them at night through the bleakest periods? What have been the bedtime stories through ages of war and plague? Icing my heart, I type 'children's literature', 'history' and 'death' into an academic search engine, and rows of old articles appear on the screen.

I'm meant to be working. There's a book I need to finish, to be ready for whatever is coming next. But I find reading these articles strangely comforting. The writing is so clinical. The tone wiped of excess emotion. One neat thought is strung after another. I could be researching a thesis, not scanning every paragraph for grand and consoling answers. Not looking for how to tell children about the arrival of their worst fear. The past seems the perfect way to avoid thinking about the future, even as it brings me back to you. For in the beginning—before papyrus or cuneiform or the illuminated manuscript—there was an adult and a child in the dark.

Adults might say the words, but children, waiting for sleep, make the stories. They direct them, picturing the actors, their costumes, the sets and special effects. And the stories make the child, filling a head with the struggles and solutions of the characters the child accompanies.

In a Brothers Grimm tale of ancient provenance, a prince sets out to learn fear. Nothing frightens him. Not midnight in a belltower with a ghost, not standing under the gallows with dead bodies shifting in the breeze above him, not nights spent in a haunted castle, every dark corner morphing into a black cat. Not even a gang using skulls and severed legs to play ninepins. The only thing that makes him so much as shudder, right at the story's end, is a bucket of freezing water.

Unlike children down the ages hearing these stories—stories typically driven by fear of monsters, strangers, wolves, God, of straying off the path—the prince never learns fear. Not fear as a thrill, as a tool, a weapon, a millstone. Neither does he learn fear of abandonment, of growing up, or of not growing up. Nor, of course, fear of death.

But to have no fear at all is as absurd as to be full of fear. For frightening things turn out to be everywhere. A loved one's body may suddenly be the cause of it. A new chill is all through our house. When the light goes off in the hallway beyond your room, the dark appears, and the night comes swarming towards us.

———

Why do we tell stories at night? To plant the answers required for the next twenty-four hours, or to forget the test that's just been? The night can wipe away loss, according to a tale told in ancient India.

Once there was a goddess called Yami, known as the Lady of Life. After her twin brother, Yama, the Lord of Death, became the first ever to die, she was inconsolable. 'Today hath he died,' she repeated constantly. The other gods agreed that 'in this way she will never forget him' and decided to make night. Only day existed then. The gods created night. Then came into being the morrow. Then she forgat him. Therefore they say, "'Tis days and nights make men forget sorrow.'"

———

You call out in the dark. As if on a roster, the two of you alternate night waking, just as Don and I had kept a vague account of who last got up to either of you. This time, I stumble into your room. Through tears you say, 'I'm stranded in my bed with a dream in my head!'

———

With the invention of night came nightmares. Folk stories are fever dreams about sex and food and gold and blood. About loss and discovery. Children heard these tales drawn from an ageless well of experience and imagination, tales that were traded and gifted, fusing with the stories of other people, in which death is always just around the corner.

In *1001 Nights*, stories netted from ancient Persia and North Africa, from West, Central and South Asia, death arrives with war, famine, infidelity and lovesickness. It can have a great fortune attached, or leave the survivors to go hungry. It comes in circumstances of horror (an army of men have their eyes torn out by an army of birds, 'sometimes by their talons and sometimes with their beaks') and of farce (a fatal hit to the heart with a date pit).

And yet death is made compact. It is given a beginning, middle and end. The stories contain it, they shrink it down. Good, I think, we too can put death in its place. And its right place is in an old tale, far away from us.

I keep reading.

In European folkstories of the Middle Ages, plague is the constant background. 'That disease entirely stripped vils, cities, castles and towns of inhabitants of men, so that scarcely anyone would be able to live in them,' wrote an Irish friar of the Black Death's sweep in 1348. 'There was scarcely a house in which only one died but commonly man and wife with their children and family going one way, namely crossing to death.'

Outbreaks of the disease, it is estimated, occurred in at least one European country a year between 1376 and 1671, and the population was halved. The plague was trailed by the printing press, with a separate literature for children emerging most broadly in the seventeenth century. The act of putting type on paper required the slipperiness of oral literature be reined in. The Puritans tried using printed works to stamp out popular tales that provided glimpses of various human desires and depravities, 'as filthy as herte can thinke'. Cinderella (whose slipper was originally fashioned of fur, then of silk, before the French fairytale master Charles Perrault changed it to glass in 1697) is on kitchen duties, in one ancient rendition, because after her mother's death her father decides he will marry *her*; thus, she's fled from home, penniless.

Young readers, being born of original sin, were given evangelical works, such as the preacher James Janeway's 1671 bestseller, *A Token for Children, being an Exact Account of the Conversion, Holy and Exemplary Lives, and Joyful Deaths of Several Young Children.* Here, readers found the details of their peers' last days, while waiting for their own entry to heaven. And that could come at horribly short notice. The seventeenth-century child had only a fifty per cent chance of reaching adulthood, and Janeway, knowing this, intruded to ask: 'How art thou affected, poor Child, in the Reading of this Book? Have you shed ever a tear since you begun reading? Have you been by your self upon your knees ... Or are you as you use to be, as careless and foolish and disobedient and wicked as ever?'

—

In the second week of waiting, Don is still in a kind of daze. By unspoken agreement, he and I act as if his diagnosis is a bad joke. A dream can feel ridiculous when you finally wake. And if we treat the cancer with a wary disregard, as if we just happen to be together in a passing nightmare, there are moments we can even laugh at it. But one day I find him in his office listening to music. He admits he keeps returning to a sonata written when the composer knew his days were limited. The music is sober and then it trills. Don thinks it sounds like synapses bursting. A brain moving from mood to mood, from thought to thought. 'It's like a mind running backwards and forwards over a life,' he tells me.

———

It was the English philosopher John Locke, I read, who argued that if children were to be given 'easy, pleasant books', they might 'play themselves into that which others are whipped for'. In *Some Thoughts Concerning Education* of 1693, Locke ushered in the modern idea of childhood—and indeed of parenthood. Knowledge could be inscribed on one's offspring as on a blank slate, potentially creating a moral and intellectual masterpiece. (I must be getting warmer now, I think. *Surely* there's the right story, a hidden gem about loss, close by ...)

After Jean-Jacques Rousseau's writings of the next century further eroded religion's insistence that children were tainted with sin, it became the enlightened view that they arrived in the world blameless. Childhood, according to the historian Kimberley Reynolds, was now imbued 'with a set of positive meanings and attributes, notably innocence, freedom, creativity, emotion, spontaneity and, perhaps most importantly for those charged with raising and educating children, malleability'.

Soon, publishers realised that the combination of nostalgia and aspiration was highly profitable. With malleability came the responsibility to shape, and in order to do this, parents were willing to spend. A German schoolmaster, on visiting the 1787 Leipzig Book Fair, noted that among the children's books 'there are few pearls and little amber, but much mud, and, at the best, painted snail-shells'. He was stunned at the range on offer:

> almanacks for children, newspapers for children, journals for children, collections for children, stories for children, comedies for children, dramas for children, geography for children, history for children, physics for children, logic for children, catechisms for children, travels for children, morals for children, grammars for children … poetry for children, sermons for children, letters for children, talks for children and unlimited variations on the same theme so that the literary doll-shops are crammed all the year round with them.

Nothing on bereavement. By today's standards, these children were more or less just left to cope. And instead of answers I've only found more and more history. (Yes, yes, I think—my highlighter in hand—but what can I *do* with this knowledge? Is there something here to help immediately? We need it now!) I recognise, all the same, the old instinct to mould. If I pick the right story from amidst the snail shells perhaps it will offer you and your brother a kind of inoculation. Can practising pain on the page circumvent it in real life?

———

If it's my turn to put you to bed, I sit for a while on the bedroom couch.

'It's too dark,' you hiss.

I turn on the globe night-light.

I remember being scared of the dark, lying waiting, waiting … Your father tells me it used to frighten him too.

At night, on the farm where he grew up, it was dark in a different way. There weren't any lights from nearby towns. The sky was black and the old house, set on a hill, was barely visible when there was no moon. The before-bed toilet trail led him outside to the realm of the cedars, already groaning in the wind. Using this outhouse tested his nerves, although the one at his grandmother's, even further from her farmhouse, was the scariest place on earth. Down a path, under a bank of cypresses, was a big bench seat worn smooth from a half-century of his forebears' arses. An old leather saddle bag hung on a nail with torn-up newspaper for wiping. He'd sit there staring into blackness.

His grandmother, who never came down to wait for him, would give him a weak torch but it was more terrifying to shine it around than to sit in the complete dark. If he switched on the light, he might see something. The Blob—from the movie he'd seen at the local hall—coming out from behind the clothesline. Or Cranky Jack perched near the woodpile. Cranky Jack was a character from a Steele Rudd story he'd read a dozen times. A wild-looking stranger arrives at a farmhouse and asks for a job. He's been walking the roads. The farmer's wife keeps asking her husband to send this odd man away, but he works like a lunatic and the farmer is reluctant to move him on. Then one day the family find him inside their house, where, having seen his own reflection in the mirror, he's taking to it with an axe, screaming, *'Me father! Me father!'*

Don's own father was a gentle man, who was first attracted to the woman who became his wife because her family appeared so much happier than his own. Don was the third of four children in a house with few books, even as he grew up on stories—stories about pioneering, and the pioneers' special dogs and horses, and the extraordinary size of pumpkins in the first years of farming, and the strange people here and there in the hills. Your father went to bed early and wind whipped up the valley, setting the trees whistling and the windows rattling. The house, with pisé walls, wasn't firm on its blocks and moved on rough winter nights. Nights far more memorable than the summer nights—this clinging to the eiderdown, while waiting for sleep to deliver him to morning …

'Where are you going?'

I'm halfway between the couch and the door.

This is the point I should exit the room. You've had the books and sometimes a private recital. I should leave you alone to put yourself to sleep—as every parenting manual advises—and yet I sit back down.

It's a kind of vigil now, brains circling the same points.

We're each listening for the other's breathing to change.

Earlier, driving with you and your brother, Gabriel had begun wailing. 'We'll be home in a minute!' I called over my shoulder. 'He doesn't like minutes,' you advised from the backseat. 'He only likes seconds.' You're his interpreter, even if you caused the cries. Over them, you added, 'I like seconds and minutes, but hours are too long.' Sitting on the couch, I'm finding I can handle hours, but not these days stretching into weeks. One thousand and one nights: the seemingly forever plus one. Why single out that last night? I imagine because it still felt like a thousand.

———

I hear Don telling you a story as I pass the bedroom door. He says later that you often edit him as he goes along, demanding a cat arrive here, or ice-cream be doled out there. Can I ask him to revise his storylines too? Can he adapt these tales to prepare you for his not being the teller? I don't think he should have to. He's still adjusting himself to his own life's sudden plot change.

———

Your father can never resist buying you various beautifully designed books, and you've shelved them unevenly. With the nightlight on, it's not too dark to miss the book's spines sticking out at odd angles.

There's one on construction with a working crane. A cookbook where you knead a squishy dough before adjusting an oven's dial. A book of elaborate cut-outs, which, if used with a torch, throws wild animal silhouettes over the bedroom walls. One that comes with 3D glasses to follow a scuba diver exploring Atlantis. And none of them are right. None of your books is the one half-flickering in my periphery with the story I need to tell you. At the end of the month, I'm again sitting in your room trying to work out how to break Don's news to you.

He does not know I have been doing this extracurricular reading, but as the weeks have passed, I have amassed a small pile of articles on the history of children's literature. I suppose I'd had the notion that by hitting the books and really swotting, I'd make our situation fit within some greater context, and suddenly see a path forward. But I've been reading this stuff as others would a manual, then getting angry when there's no useful advice.

What I'm learning is not how to talk to children about death, but how to avoid the conversation. Fairytales were once used to console an audience as much as to entertain them, and therefore the dead transform into trees or birds, or are even restored to their old life. These magical resolutions feel closed off to us. The lack of naturalism now irritates me; the wood-cutter, for instance, should only find a trail of Grandma and Red Riding Hood's offal. Why spare readers the giant landing by the beanstalk like a meteorite and, despite Jack's new riches, driving away the villagers with the stench of his mountainous, decomposing flesh?

Sex was cleared away first. In the Brothers Grimm's 1812 *Kinder-und-Hausmärchen*, or 'Tales of the Hearth', long-haired Rapunzel's 'joyful' daily visits in the tower with the prince are only curtailed when she asks the bad fairy, 'Why do you think my clothes have become too tight for me and do not fit?' In subsequent reprintings, the bawdiness was excised. So too was the horror of it being Snow White's biological mother, not her stepmother, who commands the hunter to supply her with the intestines of the fairest of them all—her own daughter. As this grit and gore got tidied up, fairy stories came to be considered *only* fit for children, just as 'shabby or old-fashioned furniture is relegated to the playroom', wrote J.R.R. Tolkien, 'primarily because adults do not want it and do not mind it being misused'.

Fairytale deaths in the modern editions are so benign they don't bother you at all.

What you find really terrifying, though, is 'Sleeping Beauty'. I bought a copy at the op-shop and had to quickly re-donate it after I found it hidden under your bed. Sleep spreads through the palace in a wave reminiscent of the Irish friar's description of plague six and a half centuries ago: 'The king and queen ... began to fall asleep along with their entire household. The horses, too ... the pigeons on the roof, and the flies on the wall. Even the fire flickering in the hearth subsided and went to sleep, and the roast stopped sizzling ... The wind, too, subsided, and not a leaf stirred any more in the trees around the palace.'

Sleep always comes for your brother fast, felling him like a palace attendant, but you use a barrage of last-minute thoughts to fend it off.

Is it the dark or sleep itself—the being out of control for eleven hours—that you're resisting? At night, there's the sense, fostered by the bedtime story, that any miracle could happen—children and pots and pans might fly—the flipside being that anything bad could happen too. A nightmare snatches a child by the reins, making him ride hostage-like through his own sleep.

I suspect you recognise the implicit horror under the surface of 'Sleeping Beauty'. REST IN PEACE we carve on tombstones, while sick pets are 'put to sleep'. Every poet ever has conflated slumber with death, and having started searching for children's books about mortality, I see this subject even where it's not. So many of your picture books are sleep polemics, sandman propaganda with narcotic rhymes: *Goodnight Moon*; *Goodnight Truck*; *Good Night, Sleep Tight*; *Goodnight, Goodnight, Construction Site*; *Time for Bed*. I'm trying to retrain myself to be less fearful, but these titles meant to ease you towards torpor now seem sinister.

After you are finally asleep, I go back to work. On the other side of the wall of my study is Don's study. I can hear him typing, perhaps also pretending to write. Our life together used to require accepting that more was going on under the surface, our surface often being one of domestic repetition. The interesting things happened elsewhere, hidden until we read the other's work. Now that's been flipped and it is domestic life that is most vital.

Before going to bed, it's your father's habit to go in and check on you and your brother. Sometimes he calls me to take a look. Your clammy bodies are splayed, the sheets twisted or fallen to the floor. The exertion of sleeping! Each night appears a fresh battle.

The American poet Robert Penn Warren was also an older father, and he wrote of standing watching his slumbering son in the poem 'Lullaby: Moonlight Lingers'.

*My son, sleep deep*
*Sleep deep, son, and dream how moonlight*
*Unremitting, whitely whitely, unpetals down the night …*
*Son, past grief, sleep*

There's always a floorboard that creaks, betraying us as we leave your room.

# Three

In bright sun, we stand across the street from the hospital. The push button at the traffic lights pulses, a *tick, tick, ticking* reminder of a heartbeat and the clock. When we stood here before Don's first appointment, one man then another brazenly lurched into the traffic to get to the hospital's entrance. We were near a street once known for its heroin trade; I wondered if they were on smack. Now I realise the men were comrades at the edge of their patience. After waiting out this month, to wait for the lights to change feels unjust.

In the waiting room, the magazines are unchanged from our previous visits. That first time, your father read the copy of *New Philosopher*, something the haematologist claimed she'd never seen another patient do. It's not philosophy people seek in a crisis; it's food and interiors. But Don picks up a decorating magazine and puts it straight down again. His head resting against the wall, he watches the door to the haematologist's room. It's just us here and, behind a small counter, the soft-skinned, kindly receptionist whose steady breathing is audible. Over the past month, I've called her at this office several times, sweet-talking and pleading and, once, bursting into tears, begging her to ask the doctor to notify us if the results arrived earlier. I've rung back and apologised for my crying, asking again if there's any news. After these histrionics, I'm sulkily embarrassed, but I've learnt the lesson: your father is a number in a vast system. His fate, and ours, will only be revealed at the assigned time.

'Weren't you planning to write a book called *Waiting*?' I suddenly remember.

'Yes.'

'Who does the waiting?'

'Odysseus struggling to get home, Penelope marking time before his arrival, all the way to refugees on Manus Island.' Don skips through centuries of ennui, of hopelessness, of politics and boats. The sea is so often a feature of the impasse.

With the pen I'm holding to write down the diagnosis, I take notes on those who learned epic patience.

'Matthew Flinders.'

Flinders, I read later, was in 1803 returning to England after circumnavigating Australia, when his clapped-out schooner forced him to seek harbour at the Isle de France, now known as Mauritius. In keeping with the spirit of the Napoleonic Wars then raging in Europe, the eminent navigator declined an invitation to dine with the French governor. The governor, offended by the snub, imprisoned him for the next six and a half years. When Flinders discovered he could climb to the prison roof and use his telescope to glimpse the sea, the telescope was confiscated and the roof's entrance boarded shut.

'Augustus Earle,' Don continues, 'who was an artist on Darwin's *Beagle*.'

These are the real-life versions of the fairytales Don invents for you: Earle was on another aging ship, the *Duke of Gloucester*, on an 1824 voyage to the Cape of Good Hope, when storms forced it to anchor off the coast of the South Atlantic island of Tristan da Cunha. Lured to the shore by the promise that this was a spot previously unvisited by any artist, Earle was abandoned three days later when, without warning, the ship set sail and, as he wrote in his journal, 'I never beheld her more!' Sixteen artworks documenting his stay have survived, including *Solitude*, a portrait of Earle and his dog on the island's rocks, scanning the horizon for a sail, often fancying he saw one 'where nothing is'. Earle lived with a handful of settlers, in dwellings crafted from shipwrecks, dressing in boots made of sea-elephant hide, trousers fashioned from sailcloth and goat's skin ('the hair outside'), while eating penguin eggs. After eight months, Earle was rescued by a ship bound for Van Diemen's Land. Imagine the relief of being on that boat, of seeing the island shrinking as the wind pushed the vessel further away.

The haematologist's door opens.

Now heavily pregnant, she's wearing a floor-length black maternity dress, and her expression is grim. She ushers us in to sit down.

Lowering herself into her own chair, she announces that Don has a common cancer, chronic lymphocytic leukaemia (CLL), but with a rare mutation—named a Burkitt's translocation.

Her breath is catching, the baby pressed against her lungs, and it feels as if Don and I are only half breathing too.

This doctor is doubly alive as she tells us she has never seen this cancer before, and there is little point looking up the disease on the internet; we won't find anything save a few scholarly articles. As she's about to start maternity leave, her colleague—the Head of Leukaemia at the city's cancer hospital—will take over Don's care. He has encountered the cancer once or twice, overseas.

The translocation means that at some unpredictable moment the cancer will turn feral, transforming into an aggressive, large-cell leukaemia, and from the late-night internet searches I've already done, I know that Don will then have five to eight months to live. Usually, the haemotologist tells us, chemotherapy is not recommended in a case like this: it can accelerate rather than slow the disease. But she has found literature documenting one person holding on for five years, another for ten. Her tone conveys they were outliers.

Later, I wonder what it is like routinely telling people the time-frame in which they'll die. If you've done this over and over, do you get better at it? Is the recurrence of the conversation any defence?

Some medical schools offer a subject focusing on literature involving the fatally ill. Young doctors are trained in 'narrative competence', or so I read on one university website. They learn to 'recognise and be moved by the stories of illness' and to 'enter imaginatively in another person's narrative world', a quality, of course, that we hope children will learn through their reading, as they try on different characters and feel what it's like to live different lives.

Now, I try on the haematologist's life: every few minutes she pulls a neat pad of tissues from her dress's neckline to dab her forehead. She's consulting in one of medicine's most esoteric areas, in between, I imagine, organising baby clothes and refining the choice of pram, and middle name. Maybe people will bring gift-wrapped board books when the time comes: *Goodnight Moon, The Very Hungry Caterpillar.* Maybe she'll set them on a shelf ...

Don is silent.

I can feel him not moving in the chair next to me, his desire to flee.

Later again, when I'm closer to finding the children's books I seek, I notice death is often personified, as it is in folktales, ranging from Godfather Death in the Brothers Grimm to Old Dry Bones, a skeletal figure in the African stories of Anansi, a trickster spider. Once our death is within sight, these stories ask, can we keep it at a distance, placated?

At the previous appointment with the haematologist, she mentioned that one of her patients had flown to America for treatment, having finagled her way onto an international trial. Oh, so we're in that territory, I'd thought, fighting for a seat on the life raft. Your father thinks this kind of thing is obscene. It's healthcare for rich people. But by a random coincidence, I'd since been on the phone to an old friend whose mother had had leukaemia; her doctor had become his close friend, and was now a leading haematologist at a famous American cancer hospital. (A fairytale sign, a sail on the horizon!) Carefully, I'd written Don's haematologist a note, letting her know that her American counterpart would be happy to give a second opinion.

Now her face curls as she tells me this American's expertise is in another field, and if anything, *he* would need the advice of her colleague, the Australian haematological oncologist.

'I get it,' she adds, her voice a hand held out to stop me. 'He's your husband and you want what's best for him.'

I sense how little Don wants an argument.

As she continues putting me in my place, I regard her with a ferocity he can't see.

This is *not* good. *Very* not good. It's okay for a specialist to condescend to a patient (the haematologist has mentioned she doesn't tend to read Australian writers), but not the reverse. It's better too if the doctor doesn't find the patient's support person an arsehole; it's important they like as much about the patient as possible. And this needs to go both ways, so that the patient can believe they've picked the right god. Don is helpless, and I've pissed off rather than propitiated the most powerful being in his universe.

'So, what do I do?' he now asks gently.

The haematologist stands and suggests we should reconsider any plans to travel overseas. Not that we had any. It was no more than a fantasy, us heading abroad with our traveller's cheques to buy more life.

Full-bellied, she moves slowly to the examination table, adding, 'If you were considering having more children, I would also advise against it.'

The caution seems gratuitous, directed my way.

'What did you expect?' Later, only one person actually asks me this aloud, later, meaning, What were you thinking, having children with someone old enough to be your father? I didn't know whether to applaud or slap this friend for such frankness.

Don has a daughter who is not much younger than me. Of your older sister, I've heard you proudly say, 'If I asked her to buy me the whole world, she would.' But for Don, at the centre of this asymmetrical family, there's the unshakable sense that he's being punished. It's an ancient idea, repurposed by the New Age, that cancer patients have somehow brought their illness on themselves due to a moral failing. Even in 'Little Red Riding Hood' we imbibe the Judeo-Christian belief that it's the baddies who die, while the good come back to life. Don knows he's being irrational. Yet in his secret musings he can't help feeling he's being chastened for the foolhardy, death-denying indulgence of having kids at an age when disease was more likely. He and I rolled the dice and now you and your brother also have to pay.

'How old will I be when Don is a hundred and nineteen?' you recently asked.

'Fifty-seven,' I calculated. 'Why?'

'The oldest person in the world is a hundred and nineteen.'

So here we are, all working out how much time we'll be together.

There's a selfishness to having children: we couldn't first ask your permission, and you were so longed for, and fill our world with such light, I might not have asked anyway. But what *did* I expect? I suppose for Don to live at least a hundred and nineteen years.

Now, perching on the examination table, my charming partner suddenly does appear ancient. He pulls off his dark blue jumper and shirt in one movement, and his skin is sallow, toneless. He looks monumentally tired.

The doctor presses around his armpit and wonders aloud if the lymph nodes haven't grown again.

It is like a letter has arrived. In nineteenth-century novels, a mysterious envelope might turn up, revealing a plot-changing great fortune. But Don's announces a disinheritance. All the world's riches will be rescinded at an unspecified but imminent moment. As a new dire future unfurls, there is nothing we can do but wait, wait for what Don calls the sniper. Eventually a sniper comes for all of us, my love, but this one is drawing closer to your father.

Soon, we are standing back at the traffic lights with the push button. The placebo button it's sometimes called. We can press and press but the lights are automated on a predetermined cycle. The little green man is allowed to walk his tiny patch for a set time, before turning red, stopped.

Don hands me a stapled printout of his cytogenetics information. Mostly it is indecipherable: *The t (8;14) is the Burkitt translocation involving the MYC gene at 8q24 and IGH at 14q32.*

'It's written in code.'

'Read the last line,' he says.

I try, understanding only two words: *poor prognosis.*

# Four

Knowing the specific reason for Don's fatigue seems to unleash it. In the day, I find him in bed, knocked out with exhaustion. In the evening, when you're home from school, he needs to disappear and rest. On the nights he still tells you a bedtime story, I remind him to press the record function on his phone.

'Once there was a farmer on a hill who found gold. He started digging, and digging, and finally he bought TNT and blew the hill up. He didn't realise an emu had eaten a fleck of gold in a creek miles away then pooped it on this hill. Too late, the farmer has destroyed everything.'

'Once there was a clever dog and a clever pig who became friendly. The pig said to the dog, "What's that *shhhhhhhhh-shh-hhhhhhh-shhhhhhhhh* noise we hear at night?" "I've always wondered too," answered the dog. And so, one moonlit evening, they set out in the direction of the sound and found the sea.'

'Once there was a sad man who never smiled. One night, his wife asked him to rescue a beetle from their fireplace and, grumbling, he did so. The next day the beetle was sitting on his shoulder, and the day after, on his hat. It stuck with him because he'd saved its life, always whistling by rubbing its back legs together. But in time, the beetle had an accident, losing a leg. The man had to start whistling to the beetle, and so he became a happy man rather than a sad one.'

I write the stories down and think, Isn't this enough? We have the perils of greed, the wonder of discovery, and the way people can always improve, particularly by connecting to nature. Can't we leave it at that before graduating to grief? We'll get to it. We know we have to get to it. Just give us a little more time.

One night in the dark, you climb into our bed and the three of us spend the dawn hours vying for pillow and mattress space.

'Did you have a bad dream?' I ask when we all admit to being awake.

'Yes.'

You were on a farm, you tell us, picking apples with your father. A farmer arrived and his face became a coffin. You struck at the farmer's nose. The nose split off and turned into another coffin and, before waking, you tried to shrink the farmer down and fit him inside it.

I listen, dry-mouthed. You know. You must, on some level, know.

And still we don't tell you.

On one of my research binges, I find an article about gauging children's knowledge of mortality. A good starting point to any conversation is learning what a child actually knows already. The developmental psychologists S. Longbottom and V. Slaughter (yes and yes) write: 'Death is a complex concept to grasp as it has interweaving biological, socio-cultural, spiritual and emotional elements.' To discover a child's degree of comprehension, researchers initially assess their 'recognition of death as a biological event'. The child with 'a mature death concept' generally accepts the following basic concepts:

irreversibility/permanence: the understanding that
    death is a permanent state from which there
    is no return to life;
inevitability/universality: the understanding that all
    living things must die eventually;
applicability: the understanding that only living
    things can die;
cessation: the understanding that all bodily processes
    cease to function upon death;
causation: the understanding that death is ultimately
    caused by a breakdown of bodily functions.

Very young children can, on some level, appreciate most of this, but, as the psychologists point out, if parents are only raising the subject because they have to, they are probably leaving the discussion too late. If The Talk is forced by, say, the sudden loss of a family member, without any earlier groundwork, that loss may be harder for a child to accommodate.

When your father and I broach telling you boys of his diagnosis, he imagines Gabriel will fare better. He's so young—and, in truth, fixed on his mother—that the shadow of this will grow colder later. Despite your front, your extra three years gives extra vulnerability, and Don dreads the look he will see on your face when we explain what is going on.

If I can't find an old book to help, surely there's a new one. An online search of children's titles about cancer sweeps up this range: *When Mommy Had a Mastectomy; Our Family Has Cancer Too!; Mommy's in the Hospital Again; Where's Mom's Hair?* These picture books sound painted-by-number, but claim to provide simple, literal information for young children. I buy a copy of *Someone I Love is Sick,* thinking it could be right for your brother. Don't we need different books for a pre-schooler and a grade-one child?

*Someone I Love is Sick* turns out to be a binder folder with pages to individually select and clip in place, spanning 'Even though someone is sick, I still go to school and play with my friends' through to 'I got to pick something from Grandpa to keep for my own … I will always have wonderful memories.' All the pages involve the illness and departure of grandparents—the more common experience of death for children—but I don't want you boys to now start panicking about my parents too.

I hide the book in my desk drawer.

There's still
this other, better, half-imagined book I'm reaching for …

My reticence crashes into your fascination with the gory. 'What would be worse,' you ask one night, 'to be crucified or hanged?' *What?* I try to interrogate how this question even formed. But it's not just you. A cherubic five-year-old visits our house with a new yoyo. Holding it up to me, he suggests it would be perfect for a strangulation.

When did our children's bookshelves come to only include bright, primary-coloured books? To exclude death? The Victorians relished reading about really gaudy departures, people carking it in the most tear-jerking ways possible. In the 1860s, a period historians commonly refer to as the beginnings of the golden age of children's literature, death was still spotlit. Books had also begun to be published which did at least engage young readers' imaginations.

It was a literary movement corresponding with the golden age of Empire, and if the books were largely free of any religious didacticism, they now had a spirit of colonial evangelism. Boys read *Treasure Island*, of 1883, and dreamt of adventure and riches in far-off places, while for girls, piety gave way to propriety. In 1865's *Alice's Adventures in Wonderland* the heroine's quest takes place strictly in her head.

If the Victorians used sentimental notions of childhood to console themselves, the Edwardians, with their picnics and punting and parlour games, fetishised *being* children.

The playwright J.M. Barrie introduced *Peter Pan* (1906) in an era when, as his biographer Jackie Wullschläger notes, 'a longing for childhood had become a cultural phenomenon'. It was a yearning amplified by his own family's loss. When Barrie was six years old, his gifted, older brother died in an ice-skating accident. (Their grief-stricken mother took to her bed for months on end, and each night she fell asleep conversing with her lost son. 'Thus began Barrie's childhood mission to comfort his mother,' claims Wullschläger, by impersonating his brother. 'He dressed in his brother's clothes, learned his brother's way of whistling, and became fixated on the idea of remaining always a boy.')

A desire to remain a child, insulated from grown-up cares, is a death in disguise. 'To die will be an awfully big adventure,' Peter Pan famously told Wendy, and shortly afterwards twelve million young men went on the adventure of World War I. The horror of the slaughter produced a host of ennobling euphemisms: the slaughtered, often 'known unto God' and no one else, became 'the fallen' who had made 'the supreme sacrifice'.

Death entered the medical miracle of the twentieth century already camouflaged. But in scientifically advanced nations, it now takes place in hospitals or nursing homes, out of view, a medical failure rather than a natural process. And, to 'protect' our children, rarely does it make an appearance within their beautifully illustrated picture books. Sure, a child's pet cat dies.

Or an anthropomorphised pig grandmother is carefully phased out. But what fucking good, I think, growing more irate, is that?

I've now stowed various books broaching death out of sight in my office, telling myself that they're too mawkish, too clunky, too abstract. Losing a pet is *not* the same as losing a parent! It seems to me that the Anglo-American children's literature emerging from the golden age has grown to be the dominant strain, and here, human loss is nowadays kept to a bare minimum. These books taken off the British nursery shelves and animated by Walt Disney have spawned a gallery of everlasting characters that everyone recognises without ever opening a page. Tinkerbell and Cinderella and Pooh Bear are constantly reproduced on sippy cups and onesies and sheet sets. Their tales may appropriate narratives from far, far older stories from all over the world—unfixed, unpublished stories that have largely been forgotten—but their famous characters live on in an immortality of franchise renewals.

Are we reluctant to tell our children about death because we can't bear to think that they will die or that we will? The problem with research is that any whiff of the present moment brings this researcher back round like smelling salts.

———

There's a fortnight wait to see the oncologist, and one evening we visit a restaurant with my parents. Everyone is talking and laughing and you and your brother are at the centre of the bonhomie. (Whatever reservations my mother and father had had about

Don's and my age difference has been offset by the appearance of grandchildren.) It's a relief to be out of the house, where the hidden news is swarming in every room, and Don and I are enjoying your enjoyment. Neither of you is bothered that the people you best love are so much older than you. Age is not yet coupled with death. Rather it's a set of physical features. Some fathers have a beard, tattoos; your father, like your grandparents, has wrinkles, grey hair.

The adults at the table have benefited from this logic. You and your brother's lack of explicit awareness motors our ability to pretend all is well. There's Indian food, and good conversation, and the mood is bright. Then I see Don's face change as he reaches and finds the first lump on his neck.

———

The illusion of control Don had, the idea that he could see the general shape of the future, has been corrected. From his study window is a view of our garden, which he has carefully planted; here there's a grapevine turned bright scarlet, but it's unclear if he will see it change colour many times again. Everywhere lie secrets and signs; portents are hidden in any drawer he opens. The fairytale model, where one picks one's way through a strange land—an enchanted forest, or an oncology ward—at the mercy of ill or benevolent winds, feels accurate. Like an evil queen, like a wild, fanged creature, this mutation in his blood is a dangerous, unpredictable force.

In children's literature, people just accept they're living in a different dimension. They move straight from the mundane to the supernatural. The day might have begun like any other; a man wakes up and makes his children porridge, he goes about his regular life only to find the normal rules no longer apply.

'It's no use going back to yesterday, because I was a different person then,' Alice tells the Mock Turtle. She'd been lying by a riverbank when the White Rabbit passed by, complaining of lateness. It seemed 'quite natural' to her that the animal should talk. Protagonists usually take talking animals in their stride— it would be more scary for Red Riding Hood if the wolf said nothing. Only when the rabbit pulls a watch from his waistcoat pocket does Alice realise she is in Wonderland. Then there are long hallways with locked doors, a golden key just out of reach. She's a giant one moment and tiny the next, swimming in 'the pool of tears which she had wept when she was nine feet high'.

Our days, on the surface, continue to look similar. You go to school, and your brother goes to childcare, while your father sits at his desk and tries to keep working. But does it make sense to sit stringing words together? Did it ever?

Even his voice sounds different. It is weakening, as if having to speak about the cancer is leaving him hoarse. There's no way he can find to discuss the diagnosis lightly, although he'd prefer not to talk about it at all. Talking about it can give him a perverse sense of attention-seeking. He feels he's telling friends a bogus, over-the-top story, and as their faces fill with pity and horror, he wonders if he'll be caught out malingering.

If he doesn't make a fuss, as he was taught as a child, the disease might just go away by itself.

Around him, another, simpler, benevolent kind of magic is being painfully revealed.

If it seems that you have only so many chances to, say, watch your child eat a bowl of ice-cream, the act becomes profound. Thousands of years ago, someone in Mongolia invented a sweetened snow, and now we can reach out in a supermarket and grab tubs of the stuff. A plump little three-year-old, made in his father's image—as shy as he remembers being, with the same dimple and blond hair—this child receives a perfect scoop of vanilla. See the shock of the rich cold sweetness, then the fast-growing white goatee. The dedication to a happiness meted out in spoonfuls (some hard-won if you're still learning to use cutlery). How incredible to inhabit delight so fully, before turning, satisfied, to wipe your sticky face on the great serviette that is an adult's shirt.

Sometimes when your father is watching one of you, he's unable to turn away.

———

Seeing a new doctor, I'd imagined, would be like starting at a new school: no one knows our bad habits, there's a fresh chance to make friends. I dress carefully, trying to appear as normal as possible. I don't want this specialist to sense I'm difficult until there's a gun at his head. Your father keeps stalling our departure, though, the way he does before a party he is dreading.

We're late for the appointment.

I drop him off and park the car, then start running. I'm worried that when this new doctor begins talking about cancer, Don will stop listening. Our inability to focus on our own mortality has been scientifically tested. Researchers in Israel have apparently conducted experiments showing that our brains regard death as a sad and terrible event that only happens to others. Cognitive defences shield us from the idea that *we* will die. And after each haematology appointment, it has become clear to me how much Don has not heard. The language of the specialists, beyond the technical jargon, is of odds, which he admits he translates to horses. When Don was a child, a relative left a form guide in his parents' house and he came to be inexplicably enamoured with racing. When the haematologist talked about percentiles, a part of Don was down at the racetrack. One of his life's great euphorias has been watching the last few strides of a beautiful mare winning a race …

I'm not as fit as I thought.

I only stop running, though, close to the doctor's rooms so as to tie my jumper round my waist, having like a scared kid just peed myself.

The oncologist is an elegant man in black leather cowboy boots and a beautifully cut suit, his fitted shirt unbuttoned one hole further than you'd expect. In his early forties, he has a youthful complexion, glasses, close-shorn hair, and a private smile.

'I observe the *Phisician*,' wrote John Donne in 1624, against the backdrop of plague, 'with the same diligence, as he the *disease*;

I see he feares, and I feare with him: I overtake him. I overrun him in his feare … because he disguises his feare, and I see it with the more sharpnesse, because he would not have me see it.'

Turning to Don, however, this man is candid: 'I don't have a good feeling about you.'

'Based on what?' I ask.

'On the data and his appearance,' the doctor tells me.

It's true: your father looks to have been tinted grey, as if an erasure is taking place.

Cancer, the oncologist confirms, is a numbers game: by his bold calculation, there's a one-in-three chance that Don's will transform into a feral leukaemia in the next year. This would be an agonising way to die. If the cancerous cells can be kept to a barely perceptible level, the risk of one of them transforming into the sniper will be reduced, and Don will hopefully have more time. Turning to his computer, he starts hunting for something special to put in the cauldron. Chemotherapy isn't advisable, but there are other drugs.

'It's a pity you weren't here last year.' He's staring at his screen.

If Don had been diagnosed then, we learn, he could have gone straight into a trial for a new drug, its name like a henchman from an Icelandic saga. Flicking through various web pages relating to medication, the oncologist tells us this drug would have been free, rather than the $230,000 per annum it now costs.

There's already a faint scent of urine in the room.

The doctor keeps scrolling, assuring us that he can access

the drug because he's had a hand in running trials with it. With the relevant PBS subsidies, the medication would come down to $60,000 per annum.

Our faces likely give us away: some years neither of us makes that.

I can't help feeling this could all be a grift; the whole building, from foyer to lift to waiting room, has been decorated for drab anonymity. We're here as private patients, not at the public cancer hospital, because despite talking about cutting down our health insurance, we fortunately never got around to it. But apart from the standard office furniture and some framed degrees, this room we're sitting in is bare. The doctor could be an actor who's just pulled from his pocket the one adornment, a little bust of Hippocrates, and set it on the desk, ready for the sick person to arrive with their wallet.

In tales about elixirs, usually no money changes hands. The heroes procure a life-giving object through their bravery, or due to a good deed done earlier for a wizened stranger. In one medieval story cycle, the figure of the Fisher King, or Wounded King, lies in a boat fishing, awaiting the arrival of a knight who can heal him. All around, his lands grow barren. He is the guardian of the grail—a cauldron, in early versions of the story—able to resurrect the dead. But he can't be resurrected until the chosen knight comes and asks a simple question: 'Uncle, what is it that troubles you?'

The oncologist pulls his chair closer to Don's and asks solemnly, 'How are you feeling?'

How *is* he feeling?

Death raises many ironies, the greatest, in your father's opinion, being that we humans have developed brains that give us the impression we're the centre of the world, something we must unlearn even as the aperture blinks shut.

He doesn't like that the doctor dislikes the look of him, because when Don catches his grey face in the mirror he has the same thought. When did his own blood—the five or so litres of it being pumped though his body—start conspiring against him? After smoking for twenty-five, thirty years, after decades too of drinking more than the recommended daily amount, he believes he has no right to feel much more than disappointment at having cancer. However, smoking and drinking aren't risk factors for CLL. There are few known causes of the disease, which is most common among Caucasian males over the age of sixty. (The oncologist, with his faint Chinese accent, has pointed out that Asian men don't get it at all.) One risk factor is an exposure to chemicals often used in agriculture, particularly the herbicides 2,4-D and 2,4,5-T, otherwise known as Agent Orange.

On the farm where Don grew up, in the rolling green hills of South Gippsland, various chemicals were deployed, all stored in drums with a skull-and-crossbones logo on them. There were sheep dips, and sprays for the crops, and a solution called formalin, a dilution of sickly, sweet-smelling formaldehyde. In the holidays, Don would spend a few days cutting seed potatoes for replanting, while listening to the cricket on the radio. He would dip the potato in formalin to prevent scab, and watch as his father also sprayed it freely around the outside of the house to kill off summer fleas. Embalmers and anatomists have repeatedly been shown to have a higher risk of blood cancers.

Your grandfather also used 2,4-D, to kill blackberries and other weeds. Untended weeds were considered slovenly, and a schoolfriend of Don's recalled her family, out together clearing them, spraying a mist of Agent Orange into the air to cool themselves down (her father having mixed it in a 44-gallon drum with his bare arm, which later turned black and scabrous). Don's father stopped mixing his solution under the plum tree when he noticed that no earthworms remained in the soil nearby, but he and his sons continued to spray it from knapsacks, inhaling and swallowing the fine mist.

As a teenager, Don took a shotgun one beautiful afternoon and went to cull rabbits. A neighbour's farm was full of ragwort and blackberries, making a good hunting ground. He liked to be on his own, and he stopped to feast on berries. That night, terrible stomach pains began. His mother rang the neighbour, who confirmed the blackberries had just been sprayed with 2,4-D. Don was taken to the Korumburra Bush Nursing Hospital where his stomach was pumped.

Maybe that blackberry-eating incident fifty years ago had led to leukaemia. Maybe it hadn't. But here he is, sitting in the bland office of an oncologist, wondering if he'll see you and your brother reach the age he was on that sunny afternoon he went off rabbit shooting.

The oncologist stands.

If you google this doctor it becomes clear that the first specialist had been right. He's a star, with international publications, and universities and laboratories clamouring for him. It also turns out there is some cachet in Don having raised himself above the rabble of common cancers, in being uniquely cursed. The oncologist is leaving tomorrow to attend a conference in Colorado. He's bought a new pair of alligator-skin cowboy boots he'll collect there, and he'll ask his international colleagues—five other world-beaters—their opinion on Don's case.

The doctor suggests making an appointment for a month's time, then meekly we leave, bamboozled but clasping to hope.

That night, I read you a bedtime story.

You pick an old favourite.

I've seen a version I love with the giant's lumpy, hairy hand reaching down the beanstalk. The Victorian-era illustrator of that edition, Walter Crane, got the scale of the terror just right: the huge fingertips are inches away from grabbing Jack, who's undisguised amidst the curling leaves, each bean the size of one of his limbs. Even the full moon in the background is made miniature by the drama. The stolen golden harp clasps the vine, still faithful to the giant who's about to clasp Jack.

In all the most successful children's illustrations, the illustrator is colluding with the child. And to small children, adults *are* huge creatures, with enormous toothy grins and unpredictable ways. Kids spend their days at the mercy of these capricious individuals, and the risk of being devoured doesn't always feel far-fetched.

*'You stupid boy!'* I give it real feeling when Jack's mother throws the useless-seeming beans out the window. I'm feeling like her right now, harried and irritable, worried about money. I calculate that, to pay for the medication, we can borrow against our house for the first year, but beyond that no bank will lend to us with our increasingly unstable income. We need a magic beanstalk to grow in our garden so one of us can clamber up and steal some meathead's gold.

# Five

In an orphanage, children lie asleep, their beds in rows. Covered by rags, they're starved of food and love before they flicker from the screen ... Your best friend's mother turns off the movie. You and your friend were both frightened by these opening scenes, and although she knows Don is sick, she doesn't turn it off only for you. By dire coincidence, your friend's father discovered he was gravely ill a few weeks before Don. He presumed he'd torn a muscle. It was a tumour. Diagnosed with stage four oesophageal cancer, he began chemotherapy immediately, and the fissure between his family's old and new lives widens daily.

When your friend's mother is not at hospital appointments, I see her at school pick-up. You and your friend dump your bags at our feet and dash towards a rolling football match, while we stand apart from the other parents as if under a different weather system. She and I had been drawn to each other before you boys became friends. She'd pointed out that hanging around the schoolyard was like being back at school ourselves, with various cliques and intrigues emerging amongst the parents. I noticed her instinct for kindness towards those who didn't fit in. She'd make an effort when she didn't need to. Even now, she slips me books that she's found helpful in a brown paper bag, guidebooks on how to equip children for a parent's serious illness. Around us, the other mothers and fathers have their problems, but extinction doesn't lurk as close. As our children run up and down the school's old basketball court, something almost spectral hangs over them.

Your friend's mother, my new friend, is trying to stay hopeful. The oncologists are managing to keep her partner's tumours from growing, but the hospital has also assigned someone to record his personal history. This hospice biographer—that's the job description, I learn—is compiling a document answering some of the questions your friend might one day wish he could ask.

He and his sister both know their dad is very unwell. The effects of the chemotherapy are obvious, and anyway, their mother is determined not to hide the truth. Intuitively, she's able to see things from her children's point of view, to frame information in the right terms without condescending.

'Have you told the kids yet?' she asks occasionally, and each time I answer no.

I tell myself we're preparing what to say. We need the right words in the right shape, and I don't feel I've found the language, let alone the basic philosophy, with which to start the conversation.

Instead at four pm, when the school gate is locked we head home for what has become a perilous stretch of hours before bedtime.

As the daylight fades, I begin playing my nightly game of everything-is-alright. Your father and I are waiting to hear how the other experts would treat Don's case, whether we need to start finding money for the new drug, and I am trying to radiate relentless sunniness. I've decided that when you look back on this time, these evenings when we are all together, you must think of it as happy.

One night, you produce a 'reader'—the school requires you to do twenty minutes of reading practice five times a week, and you've selected a small book about Hercules and his twelve labours.

Excellent, I think. Heroes. Classical heroes are just what we need!

You want to read it to Don. He's your preferred audience.

Side by side you sit on the couch in your bedroom. You hold up the book like a spy would a newspaper, your face, a fine-boned instrument, tuned to nuance. Even reading, you're alert to any floating speck of dust that might reveal why the atmosphere here is not right. It isn't as if you haven't noticed me veering from manic brightness to begging and snapping at you and your brother for quiet while your father rests. Or the fact that he is resting more and more. Now he's leaning right back into the couch, succumbing to it.

I know that often when Don is silent, he's making unspeakable calculations about what is best for you boys and for me—his swift departure or a long, expensive fight. Denial is no longer an option. After the first lumps grew from his lymph nodes, on his neck and in his armpits and groin, there were quickly too many to count. On the phone, the oncologist says to panic only when they're the size of ping-pong balls. If we're alone, Don sometimes asks me to touch his neck to see whether I agree he's almost there.

Sentences about Hercules' high bravery and superhuman achievement pass over me and Gabriel as I get him into his pyjamas. How much does he sense there's a problem here? To a three-year-old, a parent's moods *are* the weather; any little thing is deeply felt, and your brother is a child so sensitive he will hide behind us even with people he knows best. He'll walk into child-care backwards to avoid meeting the gaze of the other kids, clasping a Lego figure like an amulet. Can he really be unaware of the desperation in this room? Or is he joining in the pantomime? Children are naturals at make-believe. Throw either of you a line and you'll run with it, and take the act further.

The book about Hercules presents a fantasy of adult control, even as the thought of being an adult terrifies. All I see, though, is a mission statement. Death won't touch us as it can't touch Hercules! We will fight and fight. Just as this hero does with the Nemean lion, we will stalk the cancer with arrows, and if the arrows don't work, like Hercules we'll use a club, and then if that doesn't work, we'll strangle this enemy as he does the lion, with our bare hands!

While you're both brushing your teeth, I seek the reader out and flip through the pages, checking for Hercules' backstory. For any hint of parental influence. Did, say, losing a mother or father make Hercules more determined to succeed? Perhaps it was grief that gave him the strength to slay the nine-headed Hydra and the Stymphalian birds?

The reader neglects to mention that Hercules' dad was the king of the gods. (This kid's version also omits the detail that his father was in fact his mother's great-grandfather, who'd tricked her into a three-night stand that led to Hercules' conception; nor does it tell of the baby Hercules suckling so hard that a spray of breastmilk created the Milky Way. There's no mention of him strangling snakes in his crib, or later killing his music teacher with a lyre, or murdering both his children.) Even as I'm turning the pages, scanning for loss, I recognise that this is unhinged, but I'm desperate for some tale to tell you—and me—about rising above pain.

A children's librarian I know says that parents complain about her recommendations for older children if they feel the book's subject matter is too dark. Commonly she hears, 'Why did the parents have to die?'

A couple of reasons.

One: how can any kid have an adventure with a helicopter parent constantly surveilling for every potential risk? (I feel for you, taking off on your bike, only to have us scream a warning every time you cross a driveway.) Parents' obsession with safety and routine euthanises any story. It's every child's fantasy to be set free from such constraint.

Two: It's also their deepest fear. These books—with the

deaths usually taking place offstage—can therefore be a safe way for children to confront the idea of losing their parents, to vicariously experience a range of uncomfortable, hard emotions, including grief.

The first literary orphan many children meet is the little egg lying on the moonlit leaf in *The Very Hungry Caterpillar*. Eric Carle believed young readers 'identify with the helpless, small, insignificant caterpillar, and they rejoice when it turns into a beautiful butterfly'. The story says: I too can grow up, unfold my wings and fly into the world. A transformation that takes place in traditional tales about orphans from all over the globe. The orphan is a solitary survivor, plague and war and the attrition of childbirth hazily in their background. By story's end, however, this lack of family is compensated for with riches and admiration.

The travails of orphans were told for entertainment, but also instruction, the tale being a decision-making simulation, studded with advice. Distrust surfaces. Not everything is as it seems. Those who wish a hero harm may first appear friendly; those who look harmful or strange may become unlikely friends, even teachers. The quester must learn to ask the right questions (from the Latin root *quaestio,* meaning 'to seek'). Every hero feels overwhelmed at some point. They must manage their gifts. There will be the stirring of surprise at a burgeoning talent, and the adjustment to a new future's possibilities. Heroes remain humble as they go, brave in the face of their bittersweet aloneness.

In the morning I'm tidying up with brittle cheer. I'm stuffing the useless Hercules reader back into your schoolbag, and—this is how nuts I've become—mentally running through the great orphans of children's literature for guidance. (A character with one remaining parent can still be included in my count.)

Cinderella—female orphans typically succeed due to virtue, their reward supposedly marriage.

Huckleberry Finn—male orphans succeed through wits and bravery.

Oliver Twist—as above.

Mary Lennox—cultivated a love of nature, a secret garden, and a rich relation.

Anne of Green Gables—school was a respite, and post-World War II, the Japanese apparently included this book on their curricula due to the high number of orphaned children in their country.

Mowgli in *The Jungle Book*—truly, he goes through my head, as does Peter Rabbit.

Peter Pan—how do I put this?

Sophie in *The BFG*—Don was once a committed atheist.

Heidi—he still is an atheist, but a sceptical one.

The Baudelaire children in *A Series of Unfortunate Events*—it's because your father can't bear the thought of being forever separated from you.

Harry Potter—we need to develop magical powers.

———

I'm on a tram, looking at my phone. From the phantasmagoria of Instagram emerges an image of a child's bedroom. An algorithm has discovered the perfect grey-green wall colour, and bedspread, and bedside table and reading lamp. Everything's in harmony. Nothing bad could ever happen to the child slumbering under this spell of good taste. I wish that you and your brother slept in such a room, away from scuffed things and dusty clutter. And in theory you could, because every single item is for sale. The paint, the curtains, the carpet, the bed, its linen … Everything is price-tagged.

Viscerally, it hits me once again: childhood is big business.

I realise I have bought baby clothes and toys as if they were charms, on some level believing that the right curation of bright objects would give us entry to a paradisiacal place where you would be kept immune from harm. All your beautifully packaged accoutrements, yours and your brother's—wooden toy planes and piped pyjamas—were perfectly calibrated to invoke nostalgia. Nostalgia for a childhood whitewashed of imperfection—in other words, a childhood no one can have. New parents dress the set—the nursery—for the play they want and then start acting in all sorts of off-script ways.

At what point did I start to believe that I could control your early years so as to spare you pain? Was I intending to follow you boys around, inoculating you against being lonely, duped, lied to, traduced, fobbed off, humiliated, made fun of or made to feel ungainly or stupid? I'd be taking away your chance to learn that none of these feelings need stop you, and that one day they won't even seem to matter that much.

The book I've been writing involves people dying in a deliberately lit fire. You know this. You've met a woman who lost two sons to the fire. But maybe I've avoided talking about *our* mortality because it seemed too close, even before your father's diagnosis. Due to his age, and your grandparents' age. I wanted to hold it out of sight. If your bedroom's colour scheme remained a luminescent green and yellow and scarlet, we could stay safe in the cocooning pages of *The Very Hungry Caterpillar*.

But who actually has such a childhood? Certainly not Eric Carle, the author of this masterpiece.

That night, I read that Carle's first six years were spent with his German émigré parents in the United States, before, in a devastating miscalculation, his homesick mother decided to resettle the family in Stuttgart. It was the mid-1930s, and the saturated colour in Carle's books, he claimed, was an 'antidote' to the 'dull, grey ... camouflaged' world of his soon-to-be-wartorn homeland. The bursting cherry pie and the succulent sausage that fattened the caterpillar were fantasies of a child in the midst of deprivation. Carle's gentle father, who had filled his son's head with stories and drawings and wonder at nature's 'small living things', was soon drafted into the German army. He spent the next eight years being broken mentally and physically as a Russian prisoner of war. Carle was conscripted, aged fifteen, by the Nazis to dig trenches along the Siegfried Line, Germany's western frontier. On his first day, three Russians were 'killed a few feet away'.

I shift from researching children's literature to those who wrote it. The authors' stories are made of rougher, wonkier, more realistic material. It's a strange refuge, reading about terrible childhoods, but once I start I can't stop. It turns out your bookshelves are full of tales about orphans written *by* orphans. Over and over, I find that the early years of our most lionised children's writers were marked by loss.

Jacob and Wilhelm Grimm's jurist father, for example, died of pneumonia in 1796: after 'violent stinging pains at every breath', wrote Jacob, who was eleven, while Wilhelm was ten. The Grimm family then lost their grand house and servants and began living on relatives' handouts. (The reversal of fortune authors so often made fictional use of was for many a lived experience, penury being a precondition of much writing.) Despite their academic brilliance, the Grimm brothers' poverty ensured their treatment as second-class students at school and university. Working as librarians, they struggled financially while collecting fairytales, specimens of a folk tradition they feared would be lost 'like dew in the hot sun' as industrialisation displaced people from their villages. In that collection, the poor become rich ('Puss in Boots') and the once-rich find wealth and happiness again ('Cinderella'). The publication of these 'hearth stories' also restored the brothers to the bustling, comfortable hearth they'd known before their father's death.

Hans Christian Andersen, born in 1805 to an illiterate washerwoman and a depressive shoemaker, described himself as a 'swamp plant'. His bog was the Danish provincial town of Odense, which was 'a hundred years behind the times': the oral tales the Grimms were protecting over the German border here being in easy circulation. As a child, Andersen frequented the asylum where his grandmother tended the garden. Old women in the asylum's spinning room told him stories, he later recalled, of 'a world as rich as that of the Thousand and One Nights', a work read to him by his bookish and devoted father, of whom he wrote, 'I possessed his whole heart—he lived for me.'

Andersen learnt early that stories were a means of dark enchantment and escape. In 1816, his father fell ill, and his superstitious mother sent her eleven-year-old son to a folk healer, who remotely treated the ailing man by knotting wool on the boy's arm. Shortly after his father died. His corpse remained on the bed and the boy slept on the floor with his mother. A cricket chirped through the night and she told it, 'You needn't call him: the Ice Maiden has taken him.' The previous winter, Andersen recalled, 'when our window-panes were frozen over; my father had shown us a figure on one of the window-panes like that of a maid stretching out both her arms. "She must have come to fetch me," he said in fun; and now that he lay dead on his bed my mother remembered this.'

In 1852, three-year-old Frances Hodgson Burnett's father died of a stroke. Laid out on his 'crimson-draped four-poster bed … he looked as if he were asleep', but 'so little explanation' was given to his daughter that the death 'seemed only to be a thing of mystery'. It did, however, set about a financial unwinding that would spur Frances into writing to support her family. Burnett first published at nineteen, and her material had often been tested on her inner circle. No one 'was ever harrowed too long or allowed to rust her crochet needles entirely with tears'. Homes lost and found were a preoccupation in her work, and orphans—such as Mary Lennox of *The Secret Garden*—were guaranteed by story's end love and security.

Her contemporary, Edith Nesbit, born in 1858, also lost her father as a three-year-old. Like Burnett, she lived with her mother and siblings in increasingly straitened circumstances before publishing such bestsellers as *The Treasure Seekers* about children who restore their family's fortune. Writing was a means for these women who'd fallen down the social ladder to regain their footing, even if the ubiquity of successful female children's authors is proof of the genre's traditionally lowly place in any literary hierarchy.

Kenneth Grahame lost his lively and affectionate mother to scarlet fever in 1864, a few weeks after his fifth birthday. His alcoholic father abandoned him and his siblings to the care of their emotionally remote grandmother in the Berkshire Downs. There he found solace in the landscape, in the 'running water, woodlands … dusty roads' described elegiacally, many years later, in *The Wind in the Willows*. Having few toys as a child, Grahame went on to collect them as an adult. A friend later noted that his office 'looked like a nursery … Toys were everywhere—intriguing, fascinating toys which could hardly have been conducive to study.' (Grahame and his wife wrote each other long letters in baby-talk: 'oos lookin' arter my drorful o dolls at ome?') The author had a complicated relationship with his own child—a boy whom he found aggressive and difficult. He began telling his son stories about a mole and a water rat and a toad in order to calm him down.

Lucy Maud Montgomery, the author of *Anne of Green Gables*, claimed her first memory was as a 21-month-old, in 1876, when she was carried into a parlour to see her tubercular mother laid out in a coffin. She later wrote that looking at her mother's face, 'I did not feel any sorrow for I realised nothing of what it all meant. I was only vaguely troubled. Why was mother so still? And why was father crying? I reached down and laid my baby hand against mother's cheek. Even yet I can feel the peculiar coldness of that touch. The memory of it seems to link me with mother, some-how—the only remembrance I have of actual contact.' Montgomery then found herself a 'charity child', raised by unloving elderly grandparents.

I know this list goes on—and that it's macabre by many peo-ple's standards these days—but I need to read about those who lived through grief and triumphed. And as I do, of course, in a corner of my mind there's always you and your brother and your friend …

Only a few days ago he arrived for a playdate, and at the door you'd exchanged toothless smiles. (You share a belief in the tooth fairy, even though in our house the fairy has been leaving teeth uncollected, straining credulity.) Your friend is a keen builder and you both went straight to the back garden's sandpit and began work. You took turns adding water to the sand, mixing with child-sized shovels a kind of concrete, which you deposited in various places around the garden as if fortifying the place.

You looked dazzlingly happy, but unlike your friend, you were not yet aware of why we would need this series of protections. Instead, you joyfully followed his instructions and made each mound higher. These stories about various children's writers are my form of buttress; they're bracing in both senses of the word. And so I keep reading them.

J.R.R Tolkien's father died of rheumatic fever when he was four, leaving his wife and two young sons dependent on their extended family for support. Mabel Tolkien was soon ostracised, however, for converting to Catholicism. She moved her children to the English hamlet of Sarehole, outside the Black Country of Birmingham (a landscape reconfigured as the Shire in *The Lord of the Rings*). To save funds, Mabel became her sons' governess, encouraging Tolkien's affinity for language and love of fairy stories—tales, he later wrote, about the 'oldest, and deepest desire' of 'the Great Escape: the Escape from Death'. When he was twelve years old, his mother, 'worn out with persecution, poverty, and largely consequent disease', died from complications due to acute diabetes ...

It seems to me these histories are a hidden key to the enchantment in the authors' works. Should I be doing a control test? A comparison of the literature written by non-orphans? I don't want to. Knowing the success of the bereaved writers' books provides the in-built relief of a happy ending. And often embedded in their work is a philosophical framework to deal with the dark.

As a child, P.L. Travers believed that her father transformed into a star after his 1907 death, and her famous heroine, the protector and enchantress Mary Poppins, arrives from the heavens—perhaps, it's later hinted, from the star cluster the Pleiades. In the later Poppins volumes, Travers increasingly espouses the mysticism she had turned to: 'the tree overhead, that stone beneath us, the bird, the beast, the star—we are all one, all moving to the same end'.

C.S. Lewis also offered readers a spiritual position. In 1908, Lewis's mother died of abdominal cancer. He was at that time a precocious nine-year-old who'd graduated from Beatrix Potter and was reading *Paradise Lost* (from which the lines 'More woe, the more your taste is now of joy' fixed in his imagination.) Later he denied the charge that in his writing he'd planned to 'say something about Christianity to children' then 'hammered' it out, claiming 'that element pushed itself in of its own accord'. The *Narnia* books, he conceded, run in allegorical parallel to Bible stories, from the story of Creation through to the Last Judgement.

Antoine de Saint-Exupéry had perhaps a simpler means to steady himself: the recollection of happiness. He was three years old when, in 1904, his 41-year-old father died of a stroke at a French train station. He left his aristocratic wife and five young children penniless, although Madame de Saint-Exupéry's godmother allowed the family to live in her park-lined Louis XVI château. As an adult, Saint-Exupéry claimed to have survived one terrifying experience—a 1935 plane crash in the Sahara—by recalling the existence of his childhood home: 'I was no longer this body, flung up on a shore; I orientated myself; I was the child of this house.' In

*The Little Prince*, the hero outlines a similar schema for happiness. He tells the aviator that he longs for a star far away, upon which a certain flower grows: 'The house, the stars, the desert—what gives them their beauty is something that is invisible.' A memory, in other words, can act as a compass, a light.

For Roald Dahl, pain was warded off with black humour. Dahl's older sister died of appendicitis in 1920 when he was three years old. In the following weeks, his father, 'overwhelmed with grief', contracted pneumonia and 'refused to fight … thinking,' Dahl later reflected, 'of his beloved daughter, and … wanting to join her in heaven'. Dahl himself would experience a similar anguish in 1962, when his seven-year-old daughter died of measles encephalitis. He began writing *Charlie and the Chocolate Factory* while 'limp with despair'. The heartbroken require sugar and, if they can manage it, *frothbuggling, gloriumptous, whoopsy wiffling* laughter at the dark.

You may never read half the writers I've just mentioned. Or you may regard their books as curios, or find their other attitudes sour the writing. But the point is, the writing itself was the common palliative. The act of putting words on paper could act as a salve. Tolkien was explicit that *The Lord of the Rings* originated from his *Sehnsuct*—German for wistful yearning—to recover through writing 'that happy childhood which ended when I was orphaned'.

If the enchantment on the pages of these books has in part been generated by the grief experienced by the authors, could it be that while any reader can feel that enchantment, the works have special power for the child in extremis, whose need for escape or succour is greater? Taken at the right dose, can fiction offer a tonic? Stories do, after all, lead us into other worlds as effectively as the 'subtle knife' in Phillip Pullman's *His Dark Materials* trilogy, which cuts through the fabric of one universe into another. (Pullman, by the way, was seven when his father, an RAF pilot, died in a plane crash.)

In their fiction, many of these writers were sailing back towards their lost Edens, recasting the light, granting the land secret gardens and magical forests. A tree, for instance, could bear an elixir, a Narnian silver apple that magically heals a dying parent. The past, remastered, embellishes or disguises or even refuses the dark—often the ending we desire can *only* be a feat of imagination.

I had been looking for books that specifically address loss when in fact it's embedded in the books all around us. It's already in the stories your father has been telling you: nightfall converted to magic. *Once upon a time* as a unit of electricity, a force in itself to power us through.

# Six

It's after school. You're in your socks, pretending a red balloon is a football. To kick it, you raise one leg like a dancer before dashing up, arms outstretched, to retrieve it. 'He does move beautifully,' your father will admit occasionally, allowing himself only briefly to show the gods what he best loves.

'We have to tell you something important,' Don says.

You don't sit down. You don't yet know you're meant to sit down when people deliver bad news. By chance, you've dressed today with unusual formality. The collared shirt and navy trousers are fit for a solemn occasion, but you resist it. Afternoon sunlight sweeps into the room as the balloon spins over your head. It rises with each fresh kick and floats back down to you.

'I have a serious illness called leukaemia,' Don continues, trying not to sound like a brochure. 'It's a cancer in my blood and I need to go to hospital for medicine. The medicine may make

me sick, but,' he hurries
to the end, 'then I'll be as
right as rain.'

I try to blur his claim:
'There's a good *chance* the treatment
will make Dad better.' It's
important, I've read, for the sick
parent to not promise they won't die.

We're telling you this now—five
months after Don's initial diagnosis,
two and a half months after our first oncology appointment—because the oncologist has decided that
it is finally time for Don to start treatment. Further analysis of his
bone marrow had revealed another unexpected genetic mutation.
He is IgVH-positive, or—as I later read on the internet, understanding nothing—his immunoglobulin variable region heavy
chain gene has mutated, making for a more favourable prognosis.

This good news had been hard to assimilate. The oncologist
guessed Don's chances were fifty per cent improved, still leaving
him with a one-in-six possibility of the cancer turning feral in the
next year. The quorum of experts at the overseas conference had
voted three to two against using the new, expensive drug; however, with this mutation, old-school, state-subsidised chemotherapy is possible. A *cure* is even possible—not that the oncologist
wished to guess at those odds.

In our living room, your red balloon resembles an errant
blood cell, magnified and drifting lazily around us.

'Will you *sit down?*' Don sounds terse.

Your friend's mother suggested having this conversation while doing a jigsaw puzzle, or the dishes—some casual-seeming context to make the news less frightening. But Don and I are stiff-backed on the couch like we're still in the doctor's room.

You sit nearby as Don explains that he will be staying a few nights in hospital, and you can visit if you want.

'Do you have any questions?' he asks.

You always have questions, you must have one.

Answer them honestly, say the guidebooks given to us by your friend's mother. It may be that elements of the book for which I've been searching are already present in the old volumes on our shelves, but the guidebooks, with their bullet points and plain advice, distil the art of speaking to children about illness for those still learning. Be honest, but keep the information to a minimum. It's the same advice for times of plague or war, I suppose. The same advice when a parent or grandparent has a fortnight or a few days to live. Did everyone but us already understand this, that we should tell children the truth from the start? 'They know even when they don't know,' is the consensus, and what kids imagine may be far worse than the reality. Often, they have already overheard their parents or other adults talking. How many *sotto voce* conversations have we had in which the volume's crept up?

When you don't ask anything, I say, 'What do you know about cancer?'

'You can get it from the sun.' Freckles cover the bridge of your nose: you resent my relentless administration of sunscreen.

'There are lots of cancers,' Don explains. 'This one didn't come from the sun.'

You nod, seemingly more interested in the balloon. Standing, you start to kick it again.

Don is quiet as I run through the other phrases it's been recommended we use. There are three main points.

Some children believe they've created the difficult situation around them, including a parent's illness. 'Nothing you did caused this to happen,' I assure you.

Children may be scared the disease is contagious. 'You can't catch it from Don. You can give your Dad a lot of hugs.'

Children need to know they will still be taken care of. 'You will always be looked after even if your Dad is too sick to do it himself right now. Even if I'm busy with helping him.'

A brisk nod; you're treating us with polite caution.

The conversation peters out. Don and I spend our days with words but now we find we don't know what to say. Sentences ball in the throat and stick there. We're scared, and we're right to be scared. And you are right to be scared, and all the fine-scripted sentences can only do so much to soothe that fear away.

The three of us glance at each other, all perhaps expecting something more.

Later, I'll register a strange aliveness to the room. Telling the secret has redrawn the walls, and as the outside air sweeps in, I find I have the righteousness of the newly converted. How fine and simple, I think grandly, after all our subterfuge, our stalling, how very simple, the truth can be! Why *hadn't* we just told you?

To not have done so feels increasingly disrespectful.

But for now, your father stays silent.

There's no way to counter his feeling of pushing you through a door into a grim new reality, of failing to offer adequate protection.

And you stay silent too.

An outsider couldn't read doubt on your face. You've always been self-possessed, and forceful, to the point of belligerence, about being treated as an equal. To all appearances, you've handled this plot twist with the alacrity of those who simply accept that animals speak, and swords are pulled from stones. An ancient narrative strand has just opened up, after all. A child and a parent are thrust into a dim, inscrutable place, the role of protector confused, their travels connected to the pursuit of an object conveying immortality.

In many quest narratives, the hero is presented with a magical artefact which marks the beginning of the journey. Bilbo Baggins gives Frodo a chainmail vest made from the fictional metal mithril, a silvered-steel that 'shimmered … like the light upon a rippling sea'. Harry Potter receives the cloak of invisibility, 'strange to the touch, like water woven into material', providing 'constant and impenetrable concealment, no matter what spells are cast at it'. Lyra Silvertongue is bestowed an alethiometer, a golden compass decorated by 'several little pictures, each of them painted with the finest and slenderest sable brush', with which to steer her path by divining the truth.

We have nothing to give you other than a divergence into the unknown, the sense of being launched into a story of a different scale, and the sudden seriousness, the urgency, that marks such a departure.

I collect your brother from childcare.

We eat dinner and then afterwards go again, without warning flinging truth about.

Gabriel sits on my lap; there's the plump, warm comfort of his body, but he doesn't like us all turning to look at him. He burrows into me, as now the three of us explain that Don is very sick.

'Daddy needs to have some medicine.' It's hard not to sound singsong.

He pokes his head out, shyly regarding his father.

'The medicine may make him feel worse, but we hope it will make him better.'

Everything we've said feels abstract. Gabriel watches Don, processing his expression.

Your father sits still, trying not to be frightening.

Out the window, the garden he carefully planted is unruly, forest-like in patches.

The forest is where the protagonist finds they've ventured too far. In mere moments, the landscape shifts. The light changes. Shapes of trees grow unrecognisable. Underfoot, the mulch feels thick and uneven, and a tangle of branches blocks the way forward. Gone are the scattered breadcrumbs or the white pebbles meant to glow in the moonlight. There's just the sound of footfall turning eerie, echoing the lostness.

It would make just as much sense to tell you boys:

Once upon a time,
        your father found himself
    lost in the woods.

He was walking when suddenly
    the trees grew too close,
      too snarled for him to see a path.

Then, from out of nowhere,
a narrow track emerged.

He began following it.
He's following it.
We're following it.
Where it will lead
we do not know …

But your father has loved the bush. He's written about the silence, the snakes, the flies, and the glistening eucalypts.

He's written of the delirium brought on in terrain where every view looked identical, the uncanny repetitions that drove white explorers demented. Impenetrable bush with fallen trees storeys high, and 'like the side of a house to get over'. Aboriginal axe-heads buried in the undergrowth. A sky to mesmerise if one ever caught a glimpse.

Or, in other parts of the continent—for the hero is just clear of one challenge when the scenery changes again—there is only sky and 'treeless loneliness'. An 'awesome stillness'. The waterless Mallee, for instance, 'could swallow you in a couple of gulps like a troll'.

And he's written of the way that 'in all kinds of bush, including the most open kind, and when the sun is relentless, it is easy to get the feeling that all around something is holding its breath, feigning death.'

These are the woods
your father is trapped in.
The woods he is trying to escape
so he can enjoy them
once again.

We make it through the forest and find water.

We need a boat, and once upon a time
                    your father told you about one.

Picture it in your mind's eye.
Colour it in. Make it green,
your favourite colour, or blue,
your brother's.


Name it if you like.
You know boats need names.
Give it a sail, a billowing wind-catcher.
A cabin where you can sleep.


A porthole through which
to see the horizon.

Now picture the sea.
    Sometimes the water is smooth.


Other days:
    *The stern of this ship*
*would lift and*
    *The creaming wave*
*behind her*
*Boiled again in the thunderous*
    *crash of the sea.*

The boiling, creaming, thundering sea: those are the words of a poet 2,500 years ago, describing a journey of great difficulty. A sailor finds himself in frightening waters, and doubts if he is brave or clever enough for the crossing he has to make.

The hero cannot always sail away from danger, sometimes he has to set a course straight towards a place he wishes he need not venture. A place he's only visited before in the worst of his dreams. As he steers, the air grows cold, and the prow no longer slices through the waves. Even the boat wishes to turn around.

The sailor, whose name is Odysseus, finds he is floating into a fog.

For how many days and how many nights does he sail through this thick cloud? He does not know. 'Day and night had no meaning.' The view ahead, like the future, is blurred. There is only an 'endless clammy doom …' and slowly he realises he is drifting towards a place on the border of life and death.

———

'Do you know what I'm thinking about?' you ask me.

'What are you thinking about?'

'The cancer!' you stage-whisper.

It's the morning after telling you the news. Your father is standing nearby, but you say this as if he is a stranger who'd have no interest in our conversation.

Gabriel, going about his business, blushes when I try to ask him what he thinks of the illness. Now I'm the stranger, making an awkward enquiry, and perhaps in another language. He doesn't have the words to answer, or to even be sure of the question.

In the midst of our fog, you tell me your strongest feeling is sadness. You are so sorry for your father, that he has to go through this.

———

There's risk in every new wave's crest. The fog is concealing something vast and unknown, and as the sea leads Odysseus further, a lethargy comes upon him.

Everything now is 'infected with the greyness of the mist'. All colour drains from his clothes and his skin. Every view becomes grey, every meal tastes of ash.

He has to keep going.

His companions are nearby, but they are now 'shifting forms in the fog'. His thoughts, too, are 'grey, sluggish, stupid, lumpen'. Every doubt, every regret assembles in his brain, 'each with its own persuasive voice'.

One moment the weather had seemed fine and the next the crashing water tries to plunge the sailor right down. When the boat careens, not just the horizon, but his world tilts. The view is crooked from the weight of dread.

Within sight is the underworld. On some level, Odysseus might have known such a place existed, but not that the border between the realm of the living and the dead was as thin as mist. Not that *he* would have to visit this place while still alive.

He must go on, his body aching. Every step becoming harder to take. He and his companions now 'wading against the current of an ocean' that couldn't be seen.

And yet—like the very ill and those who love and try to follow them—he continues. Everything is designed for survival. Even our stories.

# Seven

Last year, in your first year of school, your teacher read a book for each letter of the alphabet.

*I* was for *Iliad*.

The teacher sat on a chair holding out the splayed children's version of the epic. A group of six-year-olds, some still trying not to wet themselves, heard about the Trojans surging up the beach to set the Greek ships alight. Bloody battles every day, gore strewn on the sand. You coloured in a picture of an ancient shield. Your class built a Trojan Horse out of cardboard, and held a discussion about what makes a hero. But really, past all that, here was a story about longevity.

Epics are tales of heroic endurance—and *their* endurance is embedded within their structure. Our ancestors fashioned these tales to be remembered. The word Aristotle used for *plot* was also employed to mean *myth*. The tale and its form were barely divisible. We like stories to be shapely. People could repeat long narratives of heroes and orphans wandering strange lands, their failures and triumphs, because everything was fitted to its rightful place.

The class moved on to the letter J, but I went out and bought you an illustrated copy of *The Adventures of Odysseus*—not that we got very far. The Cyclops was the only thing that held your attention.

I shelved *The Adventures* for later. And now, as Don packs his travel bag to go to hospital, and you and your brother absorb what the journey means, it *is* later. For while I've acquired various picture books broaching death, a closer description of what is happening to us is found in this old story.

The sudden, plunging fear; the seasickness.

The murky air on the border between life and death.

The plot that keeps turning.

In fairytales, the story resolves in a few neat steps, but in the epic, just as one danger is averted another can arise, making the tale longer in the telling.

We're organising the minutiae of Don's departure—clean pyjamas, and food in the fridge—reassembling the household for his absence. In a quiet moment I ask you and Gabriel if you'd guessed anything was wrong. You both say no, but the tension here had become so normal it's hard to recall your life before. The new honesty may have shifted something stale, although it has also made the house disorienting. The question hanging in the air has no answer, producing so many others.

———

Descent narratives involve someone visiting an underworld before returning to life. Odysseus travels to this grey place of dread, but the journey was also made in traditional stories across the globe. It's not only small children who like to hear the same thing over and over. Humankind's favourite bedtime tale may be this one, in which our heroes cross to the land of the dead while evading death themselves. The Mayans tell of the twin gods Hunahpu and Xbalanque travelling down to avenge their father. Mwindo, in a Congolese tale told by the Nyanga people, is a hero who chases his father to the jungles of the dead. In Japanese myth, Izanagi visits his sister in the Land of Darkness.

I've begun to read books for older children, a category where darkness *is* suddenly allowed, and notice this same ancient plot. Ged, the wizard-king of Ursula K. Le Guin's Earthsea series, finds the world is slipping into an unnatural lethargy and sails to the Dry Land, a grim province with no 'sounds of rain on the leaves of the forest of life', where the deceased amble 'slowly and with no purpose ... healed of pain' but also of passion. Once-devoted mothers and their children are barely conscious of each other, and 'those who had died for love passed each other in the street'. An evil wizard has riven a hole in this land, through which the dead escape. Ged must close the hole so the living do not languish in comatose immortality. Deathlessness has stolen meaning from people's lives.

In Philip Pullman's *The Amber Spyglass*, Lyra Silvertongue and Will Parry need instead to cut a hole in the land of the dead. Taking a boat over scummy waters, they find that the underworld has 'no true light, and everything [is] the same dingy colour'. The dead are 'shivering and frightened and full of pain', whispering in voices 'no louder than dry leaves falling', while policed by harpies. The child heroes, and their entourage, convince these creatures to let the dead escape through the newly made exit—so as to 'drift apart', becoming 'part of everything, alive again'. The only condition: each soul must tell a harpy one true story.

In *Harry Potter and the Deathly Hallows*, the young wizard deliberately lets depraved Lord Voldemort kill him so as to bring an end to his reign of terror. Harry finds himself lying in an eerie mist. 'His surroundings were not hidden by cloudy vapour; rather the cloudy vapour had not yet formed into surroundings.' Slowly, this white haze transforms into a palatial version of Kings Cross Station. Everyone, we're led to believe, makes their own individualised realm of death.

Why is it we keep telling this story?

Do we want to hear that the border between the living and the dead is permeable? Sometimes it may need to be policed (as in Le Guin). Sometimes it needs to be reconceived (Pullman gives us a post-Christian conception of the afterlife). But almost always the border can be defied for a strategic human gain. Jesus Christ, the Western world's best-known hero of epic, voyages to the land of the dead before returning to life with a gift for humanity. In these stories there's a frontier a hero can cross to exchange information, or if need be to reconcile. Surely we update this plot for the ongoing thrill and consolation of the heroes walking and talking with their lost loved ones. And then staging a breakout and, despite the peril of the journey, returning to the land of the living.

That is the tale, of course, I want *us* to hear.

Separation, adventure, return: now I see this basic, three-act structure full of symbolic death and rebirth everywhere. It's not just in picture books and cartoons, but in our gossip, our advertising, our memories, our politicians' speeches.

Part of the business of storytelling is to educate children to see *themselves* as the hero—not just the central character at the mercy of other forces, but the active hero who may find that suddenly the horizon line blurs, and yet they have the strength to deal with the changed view. But … there's a catch. In descent tales, while the heroes usually stay alive, and make a return, the people they love do not always make it back with them. At the last moment, the one they care for most can be wrenched from their arms.

This is the truth: a sick parent will not always survive, and when that time comes, each child will need to muster all they've learnt and go on.

You see, the constant retelling of the tale trains us to know the story, and to be ready for the moment in the dark when we're called to be the storyteller. Words, smoothed by time, can help people understand their struggles. The personal attaches to the epic. Like Odysseus, we are 'wading against the current of an ocean we can't see'. Our story, one small drop.

———

Don puts his travel bag in the car and we drive for fifteen minutes down the inner-city arterial Nicholson Street. Near the hospital the traffic is worse than usual. Don gets out of the car close to the building's entrance, and I turn into a side street. Suddenly, behind me, a security team scrambles to block this street off. Clusters of people wearing hospital lanyards are frowning, their eyes skywards. I hear shouting and lower the car window.

On the roof of the eight-storey hospital carpark, a man straddles a barrier. He is leaning into the clouds.

Traffic officers in high-vis vests arrive. Swiftly, I'm directed to detour and park in the landscaped hospital forecourt, to avoid the place where the man could land.

Turning off the car's engine, I sit and wait.

Hades is believed to derive from an ancient word meaning 'the invisible' or 'unseen', suggesting perhaps a version of hell that exists parallel to our own world. This poor, mad Cerberus, barking and clawing at air, is young, he's supple, with curly dark hair, wearing jeans and a white T-shirt.

*Fuck off!* he calls. And again. Each *faaaarrrrrkkkkkk!* a long, crow-like howl.

From the car I watch him scratching at himself, wavering in the wind as he hurls abuse at those below. And those below, in this forecourt near the hospital's public wing, include the city's poorest and sickest.

The suicidal man is ranting down at the dying while they stare up at him, sitting imperiously in the sky. In a grim act of public theatre, he's riding the wall, one leg flung out over the street, flaunting his choice of whether to live or not. In the midst of his psychosis, he has an uncanny sense of balance.

A fleet of police cars arrive and the crowd stand transfixed by this scene we've watched in countless procedurals. Only one woman, who is wheeling a gaunt loved one, walks straight past. She has a pursed-lip expression, as if she might be thinking, We'll take it, this life he doesn't want.

*Arrrkkkyoufarrkingcuuunts!*

No one can get in or out of the hospital carpark, but eventually a security team disassemble bollards and direct me and the other stranded drivers through a route that avoids the man.

Parking, then walking back, I find your father in the foyer of the private wing. He's sitting on a couch by reception, waiting to be admitted.

'You should see how many police are outside.' I'm awed at the sheer manpower required to save a life. 'Take a look.'

'I don't want to be a spectator to the poor man's distress!' Don's revolted by the suggestion.

We sit, half reading, the exposure of my barbarism another layer of tension.

After a moment, Don stands and with a certain sheepishness wanders outside.

This is the same hospital where you and your brother were born. Well-groomed pregnant women stroll towards the lifts, followed in stop-gap animation by couriers carrying balloons and flowers to the maternity ward.

Everyone, other than those here for babies, appears unwell. There's something about the hospital's lighting that gives even bystanders a pallor. Across the foyer, the coffee shop's barista has dark-ringed eyes; he looks like he should get a blood test. The cakes, laid out in the display case, don't seem right either. Manufactured too perfectly, they're hiding something. It's the same with the beautiful cotton baby mittens and beanies in the overpriced chemist. In the fine stitching, there's a hint of terror— terror that the birth won't go well. That's ultimately why women are here in this private hospital, paying too much to have their babies placed in their arms.

Don comes back. I don't ask what he's seen.

There are so many ways to be silent in a marriage.

Both of us should be better at waiting by now. Ever since we left this hospital holding you boys, our mewling trophies, time has bent and stretched. Little children go down a suburban street and because it is the whole universe, a three-minute walk can take an hour, longer. There's *only* the present tense. Each leaf on the ground, each crack in the footpath needs close observation. The slit of a neighbour's letterbox must be peered into, their rubbish-bin lid or gate has to be closed. There could be a puddle. Or a stick in the puddle. Or a stick plus a fascinating piece of trash. If a cat is sitting on a step, visible through the slats of a fence, the cat must be stared at, stared at, stared at … ('Weep for what little things could make them glad,' wrote Robert Frost.) And some days, staring at a random cat, I strived for this stoned mindfulness, but more often I felt only impatience. There's a glorious but brutal nothingness to passing the hours this way. Time had already been bludgeoned with irregular sleep, the night waking, then, at an hour when I imagined other people were at work, progressing with their lives, we were walking so slowly around the block, we seemed not to be moving.

When Don's room is ready, he and I take the lift to the top floor.

Most patients' doors are open. In the first room we pass, a bald man is sitting connected to a drip. The rooms multiply down the warren of corridors. All the intensity we feel is replicated over and over by the standardised mechanical bed, the tray table on black swivel castors, a lone armchair. Each room is identical, and there are so many rooms.

'It's everywhere,' Don says. He means cancer.

It appears he's been given the presidential suite—a big, light corner room—but in a country where everything's upholstered the deepest purple.

From the bag he used for work trips he unpacks the same items he once took on them, plus slippers and a robe. From the bag I've brought I pull out fruit and a bowl for the fruit, a bunch of violets and a vase to put them in.

We sit and keep reading.

Don is behind a thick book about the Vietnam War. He has not modified his reading in any way that I can see. There are no comforting favourites, or slimmer works for a short attention span. And so as he and I turn our books' pages, we can almost imagine this sunlit space high up in the city is a hotel room. We're on the break we always planned, just the two of us. Except that every noise coming from the corridor, every creak, should be the drugs being delivered.

A few days earlier, Don happened to run into an oncological nurse he knew. This man told him that the atmosphere in the public oncology ward where he worked could be so tense, he'd seen punch-ups start between patients. Everyone was desperate for a remedy. They felt their cancer cells progressing faster than the hospital's administrative cogs, the chance of being saved shimmering from view.

I don't want to distract Don now by even moving. He doesn't want to look up from the page and see the violets matching the hospital decor, and no thank you, he doesn't want a piece of fruit, or a ginger lozenge, or to think of the man directly out the window who's sitting on a barrier astride death.

Is this what everything has been leading to? All the business that fills a life—two marriages, two divorces, a daughter, three stepchildren, and years later two young sons—was the fucking and the fighting and the reading and the writing all leading to this high, purple room?

One moment it was Don's eighteenth birthday and he was leaving his parents' farm in a second-hand car that wouldn't drive straight. The roads on Melbourne's outskirts, lined with panel-beaters and bloodhouse pubs, led him finally to university—a newly built institution set in a dust bowl between two mental asylums, a cemetery and a drive-in movie theatre. The students were mostly working-class or, like him, off small farms. Sherry parties ended in brawls and he woke hungover. His bedroom was in the temporary history department. Each morning, on the way to the shower, he passed his lecturers in his robe. There was a Russian Jewish refugee who gave spectacular lectures on the revolution, and an ex-Jesuit teaching the sociology of knowledge, and a socialist historian critiquing the raging Vietnam War. People were thinking about the past in Australia in new ways, rescuing it from a dun-coloured story about wheat and sheep. Within a few years, Don had a doctorate in history, a small child and a marriage nearly over.

Time's sprint: he'd left academia and was writing to pay the bills. Not that he'd have called himself a writer; he wrote because he could do it easily. Churning out satire; fast, funny columns, or flapdoodle, he could earn a living, even as he got into bad habits, always casting around for that joke just beneath the surface. He wrote sketch comedy for a political comedian, and on the side, in a nice absurdity, began working as a speech writer, first for the state premier, then full-time, a few years later, for the prime minister. Being a historian was a huge resource for those speeches, and the crafting of them brought him round to writing with purpose. Writing under pressure—everything from press statements to lines to take into parliament—he started thinking in sentences all the time, sentences about Australia's past and its future. Governments are always trying to set a narrative. They need to tell a story about the nation to its people, and Don found that history could build the sense of a wave, carrying people into a larger tale.

If he could bear to hear his own words being delivered, he could see the protagonists of his stories being moved by the thought that their actions were not isolated or aberrant, but part of a greater pattern of meaning. Once, he wrote a speech for the prime minster to mark the anniversary of a World War II air battle in eastern New Guinea that drove back the Japanese army. A group of elderly pilots were in attendance. Probably they hadn't even voted for this man speaking to them, but Don had found out the towns the men came from, and why, in the context of the war, they'd been flying so far from home; also, the kind of plane they were flying, treacherous American machines called Kittyhawks. During the speech, he felt he could see the old men's hearts thumping. Separation, adventure, return: there *they* were, too, in the oldest story.

When children are small, parents aren't really dimensional. They're *yeses* and *nos*. Gatekeepers of sugar and television. People full of rules, many of them inexplicable. Why? a child asks. Why? Why? *Just because.* Too-cold hands dress you, dextrous fingers deal with buttons. And parents are ahistorical; their past is irrelevant. But I want both you boys to know about the car that drove crooked, and the old men's thumping hearts, and about the other hidden moments in the biographical data. Such as the time when, while camping, your father was taking a piss in the middle of the bush and he spied a satin bowerbird improbably trying to move a blue biro he'd just dropped. He followed this creature and glimpsed inside its bower. There, in pride of place among all the azure treasure, was a blue Matchbox car. At a younger age, there's the sense we exercise some control over these strange, enchanted moments: the episodes that become our own treasure. Right now, though, that feeling has evaporated for Don. It seems to him that this room is what was all the time waiting.

He and I sit expecting that at any moment the chemotherapy will begin. An hour passes, then another.

Every so often I can't help glancing out the window.

The room faces the top floor of the carpark, where a police officer is crouched behind a pylon, whispering updates into her CB radio. The man threatening suicide is hidden from view, obscured by a lift shaft, as is whoever is negotiating with him.

Later, I find myself thinking of this negotiator. How busy would their line of work be? Is there a call-out every day? A few times a week? Do they get close enough to see the scenes below,

the tiny toy ambulances lined
up in the hospital garage, people
moving around like counters on a
board game? And does the negotiator list
the reasons not to jump to also reassure
themselves? The pressure of waiting for
the sky to fall in must occasionally feel
too great. *Fall in, sky! Fall, so we can
put the pieces back together.*

Into this hospital room flow the
sounds of the ward: footsteps, doors closing, a nurse
retracting a biro, again and again. The patient next door
may as well be talking through a foghorn. Maybe it's the
room's acoustics: when he leaves, he's replaced by another man
droning on at high decibel. Trollies, laden with other people's
drugs, rattle along the corridor.

'Throw out your dead! Throw out your dead!' Don calls in
a low voice.

He's remembering reading about the Black Death in primary
school: a cart came along the street, the driver yelled his demand,
and people threw out their family's bodies.

It seems hours later when, through the window, I see the man
being escorted by two hospital staff down the carpark's ramp,
away from the ledge.

The next morning, I find Don attached to a machine, which is dispensing a drip balloon of medication. It makes a rhythmical clicking, an electric *glug, glug, glug*. His first infusion had taken place the previous evening, after I'd left, and this is his second course of Fludarabine, Cyclophosphamide and Rituximab, or FCR. I've tried to research this chemotherapy regime and pulled up fractal-like graphics of their chemical compounds. I can't make out what each drug does, except that the possible side effects of one includes bladder bleeding and more cancer.

A young, kind-natured nurse comes into the room; around her neck is a thin gold cross. She asks to take your father's blood pressure.

'Oh, I suppose so.' He's hamming it up, doing his impression of a beleaguered fogey.

The act misses the mark. The nurse lingers longer than she needs to. She's taken his mordant tone as a sign of dejection. As she adjusts the plastic bags of drugs, she tells him he needs to stay positive. Having a good attitude could be what saves him.

Don's expression is contrite—as though he accepts that those who die have the wrong attitude.

Solemnly, we both nod, thanking her for this advice.

She turns to give a last cheering smile.

*Throwoutyourdead, throwoutyourdead* rattles her trolley as she manoeuvres it through the doorway.

———

At the hospital, I wonder what you are both doing. Gabriel perhaps has a crayon in his hand, while grade-ones are learning about punctuation: full stops, commas—tiny markings giving a semblance of control. While it's standard as a six-year-old to feel buffeted by the vagaries of adults, you—and, of course, your friend—are discovering you're also beset by the vagaries your adults experience. Neither of you know about the percentiles around survival, the way oncologists stage cancer. Instead, there's just the new, daily queasiness.

For C.S. Lewis, the moment he lost his compass points came as he was lying in bed suffering from a headache and toothache, calling to his mother. She didn't come. The person who reliably doted on him was not at his side when he needed her. To a nine-year-old, it was an affront, then a desperate concern.

He lay listening to unexpected sounds: 'voices, and comings and goings all over the house and doors shutting and opening'. Finally, his weeping father came into his room and 'began to try to convey to my terrified mind things it had never conceived before'. The sounds he'd heard were of a doctor preparing to operate. Florence Lewis had abdominal cancer, and in 1908 surgery was still commonly performed in a patient's home.

His mother was a woman with 'the talent for happiness', who 'went straight for it as experienced travellers go for the best seat in a train', but as her illness progressed, she left her children by degrees, taken 'into the hands of nurses and delirium and morphia'. To Lewis and his brother, their house became a frightening, irregular place, 'full of strange smells and midnight noises and sinister whispered conversations'.

Lewis prayed to the 'magician' he regarded God to be, just as Digory begs the lion Aslan in *The Chronicles of Narnia*: 'But please, please—won't you—can't you give me something that will cure Mother?'

Young Lewis's prayer did not work, and he later wrote that after his mother's death, 'all settled happiness, all that was tranquil and reliable, disappeared from my life'. Her love became a lost land: 'It was sea and islands now; the great continent had sunk like Atlantis.' His father, an oppressive, unstable presence, soon sent Lewis and his brother to a boarding school run by sadists—an experience shared by many male European writers.

(Your schoolteacher, just out of teacher's college, is more like the angelic Miss Honey in Roald Dahl's *Matilda*. She loves small children in the way some teenage girls do, as they try to separate themselves from their own recent past. I think you love her back.)

Dahl was educated by a generation who'd returned traumatised from World War I—one master had a face that 'had been deformed by an RAF flying accident', another was a 'shell-shocked grunting bully'. What followed were 'days of horrors' meted out by older boys as well as masters. Thrust into this world, Dahl discovered the 'very fine line between loving your parents and deeply resenting them'. Grossly homesick, he would sleep in any dormitory bed facing the direction of his widowed mother and sisters. The injustice of the brutality he witnessed was something he never got over.

C.S. Lewis also came to wish he could forget the wrenched cries of a classmate being whipped, and the 'deathlike stillness' of the boys made to watch. Commonly, an imaginative child was delivered to educators and reconstituted as 'a pale, quivering, tear-stained, obsequious slave'.

Books were, of course, a form of escape, especially ones about young men leaving their drab circumstances and boarding a boat bound for adventure. (Scientists have conducted various experiments proving that reading not only reduces stress, lowering both a person's heartrate and blood pressure, but also that the reader physiologically experiences a range of the bodily sensations outlined on a book's pages, a phenomenon known as 'grounded cognition'.) Lewis would have *felt* himself on a sailing ship that 'rolled steadily, dipping her bow sprit now and then with a whiff of spray … drawing alow and aloft'. Robert Louis Stevenson's *Treasure Island* (1883) was one of his favourite books. A descendent of *Robinson Crusoe*, it was also influenced by the writings of Charles Darwin, feeding a public fascination with the sea and far-flung lands.

Lewis grew up in an era in which seafaring stories were standard fare for boys. Because the period known as the golden age of children's literature corresponded with what historians call Britain's imperial century (1815–1914), the emerging books were leather-bound and embossed and gilded, and detailed intrepid journeys with pirates, canoes, savages, and plunder in some form.

Lewis's friend and contemporary, J.R.R. Tolkien, admitted, 'I had very little desire to look for buried treasure or fight pirates, and *Treasure Island* left me cool.' Not because he saw the ugly side to these odysseys, but because 'Red Indians were better: there were bows and arrows (I had and have a wholly unsatisfied desire to shoot well with a bow), and strange languages, and glimpses of an archaic mode of life …'

These writers were children of their time, as the saying goes, reading books by men also of their time. Thus, while dealing with private despair, the children lost themselves in books of exotica that gave barely a glance to the communal despair of those people living in the countries where the boats arrived. For the most part, colonisation just offered the chance for a joke—the funny-sounding Oompa Loompas are happy slaves in the chocolate factory—or a call to vigilance about racial purity. Lewis's Narnians live in unspoken trepidation of invasion by a war-hungry, scimitar-wielding mob with 'dark faces and long beards', who treat animals and slaves with terrible cruelty. The south, where 'the stars are strange', is also a bastion of the uncivilised in *The Lord of the Rings*. Tolkien's heroes have to venture to the southern lands of Gondor and Mordor, and even further away is Harad, populated by a mob of 'black men like half-trolls with white eyes and red tongues'. If a book about sea can make you feel as if you're sailing, can a book with racial stereotypes make you racist, even temporarily? Harad is a mental place we no longer want our children to travel to.

———

After dinner, we lock the front door, leaving home for a ward visit. It's Don's third and last night in hospital, and dark as you boys climb into the car's booster seats. You two are rarely out at night and as we drive, Gabriel is stunned by how many grown-ups are still walking around the streets. It's a shock to find people disregarding the darkness, acting like it barely matters. You both start counting these creatures, before switching to a count of the children you see, for, as you conclude, 'they are more rare'.

Flushed visitors are in the hospital lift. One of them clasps a gift bag containing objects wrapped in soft blue tissue. The presence of two young boys turns the group jovial; they try to engage you, perhaps feeling that the baby for whom they bring these offerings gives admittance to your world. But you both stare upwards, counting the floor numbers as we rise, as if not condescending to notice them.

The two of you are reconciling yourselves to what this change of fortune means.

Before visiting, we went over the cancer again, trying to make the puzzle of the illness fit together. 'I still love him,' Gabriel assured me of Don, ending his part in the chat. But you want more detail.

'How did they know Don had leukaemia?'

'A haematologist—a doctor of blood—saw it. She used a telescope.'

'A microscope,' you corrected me.

'Yes.' I'm often misusing words these days. 'Something in his blood looked strange.'

'Had Don seen it before?' You wondered whether he'd cut himself and noticed an aberration. It's hard for you to picture how the doctor saw the blood, other than in an open wound on your father's body. You've never had a blood test, or seen it entering a test tube. I explained the logistics of how the cancer was discovered, that it wasn't visible to the naked eye. And how, no, no, this doesn't mean you will get cancer too.

We come to the eighth floor, and after making the correct series of sharp turns, knock on Don's door.

He says later he loves the way his sons' eyes roam around the hospital room, taking everything in. And it's true, you both enter like you're casing the joint.

Gabriel opens a drawer. 'Vomit bags,' he notes with authority.

One family member's life-threatening illness gives no credit to the others against gastroenteritis or headlice or fingers stuck in doors.

'Your drawings,' I prompt.

You've each drawn a picture for your father. Yours is a flag of neat bright stripes, Gabriel's a stew of glitter. Taking a packet of Blu-Tack from my handbag, you stick them at your own height, a metre up from the floor. Task completed, you then sit in the purple vinyl chairs, unblinking, wary.

Out the
window, the view,
past the carpark, stretches for kilometres.
I turn off the room's lights so you can take in the
city at night. We're surrounded by a constellation of lit windows.

Once, on this tract of land, children would have heard tales
about stars. Criss-crossing all of Australia are sacred stories of the
seven sisters.

The sisters were on the run from an angry and lustful sorcerer, a pursuit and flight that marked the Australian landscape

in mythological and
geological ways. Here a
rock hole showing where
the sorcerer burst through the
ground attempting to capture the women;
there a series of rocks, near where the sisters flew
overhead, taunting him with their exposed genitals.
On and on this struggle went, documented by the land
and in epic song cycles containing information on language,
culture, seasons and relationships, making the everyday world
pulsate with desire and danger. Eventually the sisters fled to the
sky, becoming the star formation Europeans call the Pleiades,

while the sorcerer transformed into the star known as Orion, which, in an almost identical Western myth, continues to pursue them.

Aboriginal Australians had been singing about the sisters for tens of thousands of years before Homer sang about 'a joyful Odysseus [who] sitting at helm, was steering artfully; and no sleep closed his eyes as he was staring at the Pleiades'.

You want the hospital room's lights back on.

There's nothing overtly frightening here—no alien-looking or weird-sounding machines—although you intuit it's not quite right either. The room's windows don't open. There are venetian blinds trapped within the double glazing, and the way they cut the view makes you queasy. You'd prefer not to stick around.

Suddenly, the nurse who earlier tried to give Don a pep talk enters the room. She's come to take his temperature and blood pressure.

'What good boys!' she cries, on seeing two children. 'Here to visit Grandpa!'

We all smile back, caught in the wrong family photo.

As we drive home, the night is awash in light. Car and tram and traffic lights colour the dark, their reflections prismatic. You both gaze out the windows with rapt attention. It's as if these streets you know so well have been recast and a secret adult world illuminated. In the rear-view mirror, your bodies are obscured then revealed in alternate bright slants. Sweeping along the road, we're being trailed by an electric aurora, and when we're home you tell your brother that he'll always remember this night. That's the point of life, you explain to him—before he dies, he'll look back and count up all these adventures and, if he's lucky, get to a high number.

# Eight

'Will we ever go to Brazil?' you ask.

By retracing your obsessions, I realise you're worried about Brazilian wandering spiders.

You stand from the table and under your breath count to twenty, before trying to keel backwards in imitation of this large, fine-haired spider's venom hitting your bloodstream.

Gabriel gets up from his porridge, copying. Your younger brother is far better at falling down dead than you. As if taught by a choreographer, his body loosens and he releases himself in segments, whereas you tense up in instant rigor mortis.

The two of you take turns

flinging yourselves
to the ground, pretending
to expire. 'I've died!' calls Gabriel. Then someone is
meant to open the toy doctor's case he's just received
for his fourth birthday, and examine him with one of
the wooden implements. I hold the 'bottle' of pills to
his lips and it works like Narcan and he jumps up,
ready to live and die all over again.

He collapses in front of Don, who is just
home from hospital, ashen-toned and in his dressing gown.

Sensing an advantage, you remind your brother that dead people don't talk or move. He must lie very still and remain very quiet.

'I'm moving!' Gabriel flouts.

'Don't speak!' you order.

'I'm moving and speaking!'

'You're the living dead,' Don notes, glancing down.

He has begun sleeping in the spare room, as though his
status in the household is provisional. In the days after the chemotherapy, this room has a toxic odour. The bedclothes smell
metallic, sour. Don is still radioactive, shedding the drugs on the
pillowcase through his hair and skin cells. A pamphlet from the
hospital advises all oncology patients to sit to urinate, then flush
the toilet twice with a closed lid. Their plates, cups, cutlery should

be washed separately. Their laundry cleaned twice on the longest cycle. You two, however, want to be all over your father. Whenever I look for you, invariably you're by his bedside, checking on him while imparting the minutiae of the house's goings on. If you can, if he lets you, you crawl in beside him so he'll tell a story.

———

We sail on, growing used to our new travels, and the conditions appear fine. Don's blood tests look good, says the oncologist, and the enlarged lymph nodes begin to shrink from around his neck. These days and the nights become strangely ordinary. He feels well enough to leave the spare room.

Soon, your best friend visits for what is the first sleepover for both of you.

Gabriel is treated by your friend—who is himself a younger sibling—with kindness, as an equal partner. Sitting in the living room, your brother wears a small, proud smile. But you older boys keep a formal air, as if trying to maintain dignity while seeing each other in pyjamas. It's bewildering to suddenly be together in this private way.

I make a comment about Don's chemotherapy restarting in a week.

'Is he?' Your friend's eyes light up. There's no malice in his excitement that Don is sick, more a relieved camaraderie.

'I told you he had cancer!' you say. You're smiling.

But it hadn't quite sunk in, and Don watches in pained bemusement as the two of you sit side by side in animated chat about another shared connection. It's as if you've discovered you support the same football team or enjoy the same music, only more electric. In a great friendship, no subject is taboo.

Your friend—a beautiful child, blue-eyed with jet-black hair—gives us advice. Already an expert, he explains the cycle his father experiences during treatment. He has chemotherapy one week, has to lie in bed the next, feels okay by the third week, and then it starts again.

His father is usually still at football on Saturday mornings, coaching a posse of your classmates, but the toll of the disease is becoming visible. This man, in his fifties, full of plans and ideas and fun, moves more slowly nowadays. After the training, he and Don stand on the oval in a painful-looking conference.

In the living room, you and your friend whisper to each other.

'Are any cancers contagious?' you're deputised to ask.

Don tells you that cancer is only transferable between a few animals: Tasmanian devils spread their facial tumour disease by biting each other.

Both of you listen attentively, then look relieved.

As a child, staying the night at someone's house is like visiting a foreign land. The pre-bed rituals are different, as are the pillows, the sheets, the mattress, its height, the amount of light coming in from under the door. Before bed, to settle himself, your friend unpacks from his overnight bag a brick-sized book.

When he started school, this boy was already reading chapter books while everyone else struggled to sound out their letters.

John Steinbeck, whose *Red Pony* was long set as a school text, recalled 'the appalled agony of trying to learn to read.' In California in the early 1900s, for him, words were 'devils' and books 'enemies'. He gazed 'at the black print with hatred'.

Beverly Cleary, author of the Ramona series, was placed in the dunce's corner, and in the lowest reading group in her class in Portland, Oregon in the 1920s. There, 'far from sunlight', she had to 'read words from the despised and meaningless word lists: shad, shed, shod, shin, shun, shut, shot, ship, shop, shift, shell … soon every school day became a day of fear.'

On the other hand, Toni Morrison (who wrote seven children's books besides her adult work) learnt to read when she was three years old. Her achievement, in 1934 in Ohio, had greater significance because 'we knew, particularly my parents, that there were decades when African Americans were unable to read because they were not allowed to read'.

Graham Greene (who also wrote children's books, five in all, illustrated by Edward Ardizzone) remembered 'distinctly the suddenness with which a key turned in a lock and I found I could read, not just the sentences in a reading book with the syllables coupled like railway carriages, but a real book'. Though he came from a family of teachers, he kept this feat a secret for months. A part of him understood it to be a 'dangerous moment … the future stood around on bookshelves everywhere waiting for the child to choose'. These shelves held 'books of divination, telling us about the future, and like the fortune teller who sees a long journey in the cards or death by water they influence the future'.

Your friend's accelerated reading—he now has a book-a-week habit—has kept pace with his circumstances. The books he devours serve up more complicated fare, matching this hard moment, preparing him.

I kiss an extra child goodnight, asking first for his permission.

Neither of you realise you're meant to do anything but sleep. As I close the door you close your eyes, and the room is silent.

———

Your friend's predictions prove true: just as Don starts to feel better, it is nearly time for the treatment again.

One morning, I get up early to work—I'm in the last throes of my book, correcting the typeset pages. When I return to our bedroom, I find you and your brother in our bed on either side of your father. The night before, you put yourself to sleep working out how many letters, then how many syllables, different words contain, and now Don is giving you more words to spell.

'Tired,' he suggests.

'T-i-r-e-d.'

'Stressed.'

'S-t-r-e-s-s-e-d,' you oblige.

'Happy,' I insist. The three of you look content lying there together. There's a barnyard warmth to small bodies packed in close.

You groan. 'That's too easy.'

'Get up! Arise!' Don commands, flinging back the bedclothes.

And you spell these words correctly, the day and its parts assembling before you. You're fitting out the world. And Gabriel too: 'A "p"!' he calls out while we're driving, thrilled if he spots a letter he can recognise. 'A "t"!'

As you gain new knowledge, though, some of it is painful. Your friend's mother overhears the two of you talking. You are explaining that Don will be 'right as rain' by February, the very words he used.

'I wouldn't be too sure of that,' your friend advises, now the voice of experience.

The reality of this switches on. With a new chill running through the days, spiders are the least of your fears. 'It's a race to see whose father dies first,' you tell me grimly.

———

On a quest, the hero's most terrifying confrontation is with a monster.

Pulling into an unknown, perhaps unnamed, harbour, there's a sense of disquiet. A need to keep glancing over one's shoulder. A shiver sets in, hard. This threat can be sensed before it is seen: the monster's calling card is the atmosphere of dread.

Next comes hair-standing-up-on-neck, stomach-falling alarm. The nothing-quite-rightness morphing within seconds to breath-less panic as the hero computes the existence of true horror. Living, breathing, moving horror! Wherever it lurks is too close and yet it's coming closer.

Da-DUM-
da-DUM …

A monster's features are unlike
anything seen before. Or, if they're recognis-
able, they're familiar only in a distorted, belief-defying way. The
monster resists classification. An emissary from the unknown, its
molecules are made of your terror.

Da-DUM-da-DUM … as if a heart knows it might soon be
stopped.

Pray you see it before it sees you. Pray that when it comes you
can make yourself move. Its fangs could reach your jugular faster
than thought. The monster seeks to annihilate. Maybe it will
eat you, maybe not. But it wants you vanquished, and it can't be
reasoned with—that's why it's a monster.

For the foul-smelling, leather-winged cliff-ghasts trying, in *His Dark Materials*, to kill Lyra and Will, it's nothing personal. Tolkien's Watcher in the Water doesn't particularly care that it's Frodo—bearer of the ring—about to be drowned in its luminous tentacles. The Basilisk, a giant serpent, and Aragog, a giant spider, are both unmoved by Harry Potter's powers as they try to eat him. They don't care about the boo-hoo fact that he was orphaned and raised by unloving relatives; he's just a meal to them. The monster tries to reduce heroes' struggles and bravery, their *stories*, to no more than a feed to be shat out.

Likewise, the cancer cells are indifferent. It's irrelevant whether the patient is funny or charming or insightful or has small children …

And so Don turns up for his next treatment to the hospital's oncological infusion room, a tight, bunker-like space. He's an outpatient this time, sitting in one of the oversized grey vinyl chairs lining the walls. Rolling up a sleeve, he presents his wrist to the nurse, her blue gown resembling a Hazchem suit.

There's the snap of the nurse's gloves, then the sound of plastic tearing as out of a sealed bag comes the cannula, and from another sealed bag the drugs. The debris is quickly tossed into bins for either clinical or cytotoxic waste. Don is quiet, sombre as he's hooked up to the drip.

Curtain rails run along the ceiling. If a patient vomits, a blue veil is swiftly drawn around them, their noise partially muffled by a morning television program advertising hair-loss products—the irony—and also a portable air-conditioning unit to drag around like a belligerent pet.

The saline flush is cold in Don's veins, and he shivers as the level in the bag moves rapidly down.

'It's a drench,' he says, astounded by the sheer volume.

I'm next to him on an office chair, and around us, in the other grey seats, sit men and women old and young. Some are obviously far sicker than your father. It's a jolt to see people in their forties, and even more so their thirties or twenties. A young bald woman wearing a woollen beanie smiles at me, and I force myself to smile back, but too late to hide the shock.

On a wall nearby is a poster a nurse has pinned up to add some cheer. It shows a window, shutters thrown open, looking onto a Mediterranean beach. There's turquoise water and bright yellow sand. The sand is covered in colourful deckchairs. Here's the promise of a paradise, but something doesn't feel right. I realise each deckchair sits empty. The scene after a disaster has struck.

It's no secret that some of the patients in this room will not be saved by the drugs to which they're now connected. Their cancer cells will continue growing and dividing, destroying healthy body tissue. The gamble of treatment won't pay off, even though these people may be no less virtuous or brave than those who will survive—unlike in stories, where it's the hero's less valiant comrade who doesn't make it back.

As the patients await their fate, it's distinctly possible to understand cancer through a scientific filter, as a rogue gene in a universal cycle of decay, while also feeling oneself to be in a battle with a monster, and the scariest form of monster—the one that's inside us. The hero, too, can find they're harbouring their own enemy: one glimpse in a cracked mirror and with terrible clarity they see a part of themselves that's turned rank and traitorous.

Patrick Ness's breathtaking *A Monster Calls* (2011) offers an appalling monster created by a parent's illness. The book opens with thirteen-year-old Conor in the midst of a recurring nightmare. He's woken by an apparition born of a neighbourhood yew tree with a 'huge, twisted, branch-wound hand', 'raggedy teeth made of hard, knotted wood', and a 'mouth roaring open to eat him alive'. This monster seems to know that Conor finds the ending of his nightmare unspeakable.

The bark and needles of the yew tree are used in drugs to treat breast, ovarian and lung cancers, but the monster has not come to heal Conor's ailing mother. It instead works on Conor. By day, the boy feels abjectly different from his classmates, and the kindness of well-meaning teachers only separates him further from his peers. By night, Conor hears his weakened mother vomiting, and reads the half-truths she and other adults serve up in the name of 'protecting' him. Only the monster, an untamed force, is straight. It tells Conor three vivid tales, explaining, 'Stories are wild creatures' which 'chase and bite and hunt'. In return, the monster demands one true tale of Conor, who discovers that the monster is his own distorted self, born of lonely rage at the certainty of being abandoned. In telling the monster the truth of his dream—one that reveals his fatigue with his mother's disease, the wish that it might end—he frees himself from annihilating shame.

In the infusion room, the last of three bags of drugs empties.

We wait as Don is unhooked from the drip, then, gathering our things, exit as quietly as from a church service.

I'd expected the mood in there to feel gloomier, but despite what people were dealing with internally, there was a strange serenity as they sat in oversized chairs, receiving drugs as a form of chemical benediction.

In the hospital corridor, I comment on the calm.

'It's the proximity to death,' Don reckons. He's recalling the sensation of being with a friend who was very near to dying. There was such a thin scrim, he could easily have passed through with this person he loved.

Friends lend us their house in Sydney for the school holidays. We book flights unsure if Don will be well enough to travel, but the day arrives and we all make the journey without incident.

The house has a sweeping veranda facing onto the sea. A real sea, with waves rolling in and out. Not like the poster pinned to the wall in the infusion room. I lead you and your brother down an overgrown path to the sand, true sand. People are paddling, sunbathing. There is no Cyclops here.

But when a child shits in the shallows, a terrible sea creature blooms, spreading through the water faster than shame.

———

The four of us catch a bus the next day to Circular Quay, then a ferry around the harbour. Boats give the instant sense of a bigger world. We sit on the deck, our hair blowing in the salted air, imagining the water giving passage to other places.

Here it comes on the horizon—this white-shell palace from postcards and television advertisements. Awed, you roam around the ferry, taking in the Opera House's different facets, the unexpected angles.

Your father is admiring your brother, who is asleep on his lap. ('A sleeping child gives me the impression of a traveller in a very far country,' wrote Ralph Waldo Emerson.) But your eyes are everywhere and the questions keep coming, not just about what you

see, but questions that half
flummox me. Over the past few weeks,
you've asked, 'What do you think is more
important to a storybook, the words or the
pictures?' And, 'What does guilty mean?'
When you heard me saying someone had
had a hard life, you asked, 'Will I?' And recently,
Gabriel has started joining in: 'Is a dog still a sausage dog if it's
not eating sausages?'; 'A chair has legs but can it walk?'

Very young children live in a seething, unpredictable place.
They famously ascribe feelings to clouds, waves, a boat, basically
anything that moves. Objects that are seen for the first time, or
aslant, seem like they could potentially come to life: a shiver-
inducing idea, as the authors of fairy stories understood. But this
childish instinct persists, doesn't it, often for longer than many
of us care to admit?

The Brothers Grimm believed that the poetic 'animation
of all nature' they recorded in folk stories—as well as in old
expressions, superstitions and rhymes—comprised fragments of
an older belief system. This trove, highlighting the secret life of
nature, was, they surmised, an inheritance from Pagan times.

Actually, the belief that all of nature has a life force is far
more ancient. Many indigenous cultures, including in Australia, consider all the natural things which are visible from, say,

the deck of this ferry—rocks and water and clouds—to have an interlocking consciousness. And you are dazzled by all you see, as if you believe this too.

We disembark and, weaving through the other tourists and the blood-eyed seagulls, we walk up the Opera House's terraced steps.

You touch one of the million yellowing white tiles and shake your head. It's too much to absorb.

I take a photo of the three of you, the gleaming nacre of the arches in the background.

Your father's arm is around you, and your arm is around your brother. You both look nautical, wearing shades of blue with fresh haircuts. You're squinting into the light, a broad smile showing off new front teeth, while Gabriel wriggles into different poses, head bowed. Don looks progressively more strained in each shot. He is neutropenic: he has a dangerously low white-blood-cell count and is vulnerable to infection, but we're chemotherapy novices, hanging out at the city's most crowded site. As I press the camera button, I see him waver like he's about to tip over.

We have to get back to the house.

The two of you are pulled from the excursion into a taxi, which lurches through the winding streets, on and on. We had ventured too far; we pretended everything was alright when it wasn't, and now this car keeps accelerating then jerking to a sudden halt.

Don's presence has started to feel like the beginning of an absence. Even in the car's front seat, he's somewhere else.

Somewhere unreachable, just trying to concentrate on staying alive. I want to haul him back to us, to shake him, or use that comic hand slap that brings a person round in movies. But I'm nervous to touch him: after the chemotherapy his nerve endings are more sensitive, small jolts leave him tender. It is more comfortable for him to sleep alone, and yet what if these are our last nights together? These thoughts judder on—what if this is the last time we're all on holiday? What if that was the last photo next to a landmark?

The epic hero has to learn to control fear.

J.K. Rowling introduces us in the Harry Potter series to a subtle terror called a Boggart. Assuming the form of whatever frightens a person most, this shapeshifter likes 'dark, enclosed spaces … [w]ardrobes, the gap beneath beds, the cupboards under sinks', and Professor Lupin instructs Harry's class on the spell to repel one: '[T]he thing that really finishes a Boggart is laughter. What you need to do is force it to assume a shape that you find amusing.'

One pupil imagines the teacher he fears in his grandmother's clothes. Harry's fear, however, takes the form of a Dementor (a monster, Rowling has claimed, which was inspired by her own experience of depression and grief. As a teenager, Rowling watched her mother's deterioration by multiple sclerosis, a disease that killed Ann Rowling at forty-five.) Dementors exist in 'the darkest, filthiest places'; sustained by 'decay and despair, they drain peace, hope and happiness out of the air around them'.

In a show of advanced wizardry, Professor Lupin must instead teach Harry to protect himself by conjuring a Patronus, or spirit-guardian. With intense focus, the young wizard recalls a moment of uncomplicated joy, and watches as from his wand a 'gleam comes through' and a luminous silver stag erupts, a totem of his deceased father. This Patronus, a defensive charm and symbol of hope, can only be mustered by those with exceptional skill.

In the taxi's backseat, you and your brother are weary, buffeted by the car ride and your parents' shifting moods. I can understand the logic of reimagining a fear as something absurd—so many picture-book monsters are revealed by story's end to be dimwitted or even good-natured, rather than frightening. But there's no way to turn a child's grief into something to be laughed at. Instead we have to try to do joyful things, or find joy in the old things, and store up the memories for summoning a radiant protector.

———

For the rest of the holiday, Don mostly stays in bed. He needs to rest and so the three of us head off without him to explore the city. As is always the case now, you tell your father before we leave each day that you love him. Even then, I see you hesitate to walk away. Gabriel handles the moment with pragmatism, heading straight to another waiting taxi, but you admit to feeling sad thinking of Don all alone while we're out having fun.

Your father looks relieved we are leaving, his fingers twitching to close the door on us.

———

'If one day you have a family of your own,' I say, 'you'll understand. Dad isn't lonely. He enjoys having some time to himself.'

Our first stop is publishing-related. We drive out to an online bookseller's warehouse. In a front office, I sign copies of my newly printed book, while you boys steadily make your way through what had been a decorative bowl of lollies. Then we're each given a hardhat and shown inside the warehouse, a vast concrete hangar animated by forklifts and conveyer belts, and workers in high-vis vests riding motorised scooters to locate people's desired books. Steel-grilled shelves stretch to the storeys-high ceiling, although sport stars' memoirs and various bestselling cook and diet books, I notice, are on a lower set of shelves close to the conveyer belt. The books that don't sell will be returned to the publisher to be pulped. Boggarts and Dementors surround us.

Trailing lolly wrappers, we escape into the city. We're trying for joy, but at the museum and the art gallery, your father's absence grows more pronounced. The *unlivedness* of it. All the things he and I thought we had years to do and kept pushing into an imaginary future—these things might not be.

At the Sydney Aquarium, the cruddiness of the tanks' construction holds more menace than any circling shark. The place is crowded. Children and parents jostle each other in a faux grotto. We gaze into tanks set in rock-like polystyrene. There's the smell of mould. Grey nurse sharks glide round and round, resembling goldfish in a too-small bowl. That downward slant of their jaw—it's as if, aghast, they're thinking, Four hundred and twenty million years of evolution for this?

You're more likely to remember us watching David Attenborough's *Blue Planet*. Previously you've demanded the four of us sit together in the dark to spy on this liquid world. Each shot is a phosphorescent magic act: in breeding schools, the tentacles of opalescent squid turn red as they embrace. Then, a bright slug chases another slug by sliding along its trail of slime. Then thousands of tiny bubbles hatch, each bubble turning a flesh colour, morphing into a crab with bulbous, turquoise eyes. One crab's older version is a seemingly indestructible tank with robotic claws. But what makes these unspooling images so vivid is the edge of terror. An octopus looms. It is the voluminous cape of the Reaper, just threat, disembodied threat. This bodyless hitman sweeps through the sea, and it steals the crab's life, of course, while we sit watching, transfixed.

———

We return to Melbourne to find the walls of our house closing in. It is much smaller than the one we've just visited. Out the windows, the views are mostly of paling fence, not the sea.

Gabriel has at least stopped his game of playing dead everywhere. Perhaps by acting out his own expiration, he's come to some accommodation with the concept. One night, as I struggle to get him into his pyjamas, he says plainly, 'I'm going to die.'

My head is full of other things.

'Everyone will.'

'Everyone on earth?'

'Everyone on earth.'

He lists those in our house and again
I confirm our mortality.

'But how does it happen?' he continues.

Why these philosophy sessions when the pyjama
arm-holes are so tight, the leg-holes so cavernous?
With the pressures of work and home, the days are
compressed further. I'd chosen not to delay my
book's publication partly to have a clear schedule in
case Don's condition worsened. But with publication
comes interviews, and events, and despite my parents
helping us more and more, I'm careening through
the days. At night, even getting Gabriel into
bed has a deadline—although what
a word—and his limbs keep turning the wrong way.

'How do we die?' The question
offers the perfect opening. The one that
I've been looking for, but I take it as
just another way of him stalling
bedtime.

'You stop breathing and then you go away,' I snap.

He ponders this. 'I saw a dead fly and its body didn't go away. Because it was small?'

'The fly went away in the end.'

'Do you know what I'm talking about?' he asks simply, fixing me with a gaze that speaks of something profound.

I don't know, but I do; and his expression breaks me from my frenzy.

'Once I was taking Tobias to school and I saw a dead bird. It's sad for the bird because it can't fly. It's sad because it can't eat worms anymore.'

'Yes. It is sad.'

The strangeness of seeing one's own features and mannerisms, or one's partner's (or partner's mother's) flickering across a smaller face. The face of someone who can knock me out with his steady sweetness. How could I have thought we'd just skate through this experience with Gabriel unconscious? I'd been basking in his seeming lack of awareness when, in his quiet way, he honed in on life's essential dynamics. Children have to find a way to get by with whomever they're dependent upon, even though these people may

keep changing plans, and rules, and demeanour.
An adult glances at a work email on a phone and
suddenly she's angry with the child who was just trying
to talk about birds and worms.

Much children's literature revolves around the awfulness of
adults. At boarding school, Roald Dahl learnt that 'a grown-up
was a grown-up and all grown-ups were dangerous creatures'.
Or, as Antoine de Saint-Exupéry put it in *The Little Prince*,
'I have lived a great deal among grown-ups. I have seen
them up close. That has not much improved
my opinion.' Maurice Sendak dealt with
the 'real monsters of my childhood',
his elderly relations, by making them
more monstrous. He grew up in the
shadow of the Holocaust, his father's
extended family having all been
killed. His mother's Jewish
relatives, safe in America,
were not, however,
a comforting
presence.

They had 'bloodshot eyes', bad teeth, 'hair curling out of the nose', and would tell him he looked 'so good we can eat you up', thus becoming the wild things of his famous picture book. For him, boyhood was spent 'being a creature without power, without pocket money, without escape routes of any kind'. He was taken to see *Peter Pan* and 'detested it', finding the 'idea that anybody would want to remain a boy ... a conceit that could only occur in the mind of a very sentimental writer ... The wish is to get out.' And yet, 'getting out' required awaiting a horrible new fate, for 'to become an adult was to become another dreadful creature'.

We do a good job of acting benign. There's faux gaiety each morning at the childcare centre's doorway. Standing inhaling the vegetal smell of the place, it's better not to make eye contact with the other parents (mothers usually) and see the murky feelings reflected back. How can I be relieved to say goodbye to a creature whose small hand reaching up for mine gives an electric shock of love? A creature whose crowning Fibonacci spiral of hair I worship? Women slink off from the centre hoping that by day's end the child will have forgotten the fight they've just had over socks, or cereal, or seatbelts.

But outside the gates one morning, a woman admits to me that she finds herself morphing each day into an unpredictable, explosive person, the sort of person she would deeply disdain in any other context, and I feel like I could be looking in a mirror.

We tell children stories of heroes taming monsters as lessons in civility, but as I read to you about Max commanding the Wild Things to 'BE STILL!' I wonder who this is really for. Adult or child?

———

Soon Don is back in the day oncology room. It comes with a mild hallucination of a cow yard. He could be on the farm amidst, as he's put it, the 'cypresses and gums baking in the sun or stewing in the damp'.
The clear bags of drugs become cow's udders.

He loves the nurses here, their matter-of-fact warmth and skills, the life and purpose they give the room, but the calculated violence of his father's axe swing is there as they insert the cannula. Another patient, a man arrived from the country who, he learns, is staying alone in a rooming house, bleeds like a stuck pig when a nurse tries to find a vein.

In Don's childhood, death was not discussed—not the death of humans, at least. He was eight years old and in grade two when the friend he sat next to in class was run over and killed by a milk truck from the local butter factory. The schoolkids were lined up outside the church to watch the little coffin pass. And that was that. Nothing more was said, either at home or in school, about the empty desk next to his. He might have half heard adult murmurings about a widely held suspicion that the truck's driver had been drunk. But the boy was from a poor family, and he—and his cause of death—were buried simultaneously. Death was something to be got over by dinnertime, just as cancer was a word coughed into the hand.

'He had a growth,' people would murmur of the sufferer, as if clearing their throat. When an upright and respected citizen shot himself behind one of the town's churches, the story was he also had 'a growth'. Mental illness was no less taboo than cancer. Children, meanwhile, were expected to learn death's mysteries much as they learned those of sex—from the animals. On the farm, animals died regularly, without eliciting much comment. It was not so different with people, except for the vague bribe, *Behave well and you'll go to heaven.*

An alarm sounds when a bag of medication has emptied.

As each patient leaves, the nurses wipe down the vinyl chairs with disinfectant, ready for the next person.

It's hard when sitting tied to the drip, not to think of mistakes, of wrong turns. Regret is a kind of demon, at first slow-footed, then a thing of speed. There are years of his life Don would like back. Years he thinks he wasted, spending too many nights in bars, then too many days hungover. He'd fallen in with an older crowd of heavy-drinking writers and artists. Friends died young, everyone else crashed around, and so did he: guilty to have left his first marriage, and later to have broken up the marriage of the woman who would become his second wife, before that too ended in flames; in love, he wishes he'd stayed either longer or not as long. This life of his was unrecognisable to his parents.

As a boy he'd been happiest walking around the farm. Whenever it rained, he followed the rivulets that emerged in the paddocks. These twisting watercourses, two feet wide, rushed between the hillsides; he'd walk up and down alongside them, to dream, to think. Wet weather transformed the land, revealing its shimmering secrets. And there were moments, later, writing as an adult, when he felt that same pleasure. The same freedom of ranging around in his head.

Poowong, the name of the town where he went to primary school, he found was derived from an Indigenous word meaning 'carrion'; and Korrumburra, where he went to high school, meant 'blowfly' or 'maggot'. While death was kept quiet in Don's family, they were living in an area where generations of Aboriginal people had incorporated the cycles of life into their cosmology. There would have been songs and stories about decomposition, a reflection of everyday life. Over the hills, Jindivik, the place where Don's father had spent his childhood, was said to mean 'decay', or sometimes 'disappear', or 'irrecoverable, lost for good'.

As a young historian, it had filled Don with rage that white Australians denied the violence of the frontier, the massacres that had happened not far from the place where he'd ambled. Such violence occurred in all settler societies around the globe; why could the facts not be faced here? The old school of historians, raised on those gilded and embossed boys' volumes about canoes and islands, wrote as if unable to free themselves from a storybook sense of adventure and valour, of intrepid explorers and civilisation's march; they thus created for themselves a deathless history.

The 'natives' in Victorian and Edwardian children's literature are an undefined mob, barely given human status, and therefore part-monster. In one of the most beloved Australian children's books, May Gibbs' *Snugglepot and Cuddlepie* (1918), the villains are the Big Bad Banksia Men, racist caricatures of Aborigines transposed onto banksia flowers, who constantly try to steal white, eucalyptus-nut children. Back and back these monsters go, rewinding to whatever fear of an unknown force or unknown group first kept people awake at night, a legacy begetting new monsters. The real monstrosity, though, is to destroy, or *de-story*, another culture.

How, in stories, does one stop a creature set on annihilation?

By finding the right words, by casting the right enchantment. The idea of language being an animated, animating force is a prehistoric one. Some linguists suggest that *Abracadabra* may come from the Hebrew for 'I will create as I speak', or from Aramaic: 'I create like the word.' In Indigenous Australian culture, sacred words are chanted or sung, as they have been for however many tens of thousands of years. Words hold power. Early humans' ability to describe their environment was a vital tool for survival, and the extension of this, anthropologists have argued, was the belief that 'a verbal act' could affect the environment, sanctifying it and the people in it.

Just as wizards, by naming things precisely, can control them, a writer who finds the right set of words for what grieves them can pin the grievance down, fixing it in place. Language is a trap we build to catch meaning. The correct description stops time and saves a slice of it. Sometimes this is the only form of control, the only spell of hope for the future. Describing *perfectly* what one finds monstrous is therefore essential. The hero tames the monster by calling it by its true name.

At school, you and your friend spend lunchtimes writing a book called 'The Haunted House'. Both your houses are currently haunted. (When we encounter a dying person, on some level we feel we're also encountering their ghost.) Each day, you write the words and your friend draws the pictures. His mother has told her children that their father's body might not be strong enough to keep fighting for much longer. Every twenty-four hours has become hard-won. I offer to have your friend to stay with us whenever it would be helpful, but she wants to keep their family together while she can.

You and I are walking home from school when you tell me you wish you could live with all your family and your friend in a house with a lemonade fountain, and a candy bar, and a movie theatre, a pool, a catapult, a soccer field, a drum kit, and where no one ever dies.

# Nine

In many epics, when heroes are away questing, their homeland falls into disarray. An ill wind passes over the shire. The skies are bleak, nothing grows. But outside, our garden is now in lush spring.

When we moved to this house, Don razed the old concrete vegetable beds and haphazardly positioned fruit trees and began again. There are now hundreds of different plants on our suburban block. Plants to attract birds. Plants to give shade. Plants hidden as surprises. Your father likes putting things in the ground that do more than one thing—trees that flower or have varying foliage, bark that peels back revealing an unlikely reptilian marking. Under the trees are other changeable things: red-hot pokers, or kniphofias, in amethyst and apricot; globe-shaped alliums, intricately engineered with miniature petals; hummingbird mint, its tubular flowers looking like nectar-filled flagons; blue haze; spiky, metallic sea holly; sweet-smelling creepers; and white and indigo crocuses, emerging, as they do in *The Secret Garden*, 'like magic: a little crack where a whole new world was about to open and transform'. After winter, our garden is a whole new sensuous world, but in truth it's one I've tended to move through, giving minimal attention.

Mainly I am conscious of a battle for supremacy raging between your father and your football. You would prefer unimpeded lawn, more room to play. The Vale of Tears is how Don describes the patch of grass that does exist. His sons get into nightly stoushes over who's scored a goal, the ball having broken longed-for growth on a rare plant, with Don typically going down on hands and knees to replant what's been trampled out.

By late October, though, he doesn't feel well enough to work in the garden at all. He is halfway through the chemotherapy program, with the side effects becoming cumulative. He's nauseous and dizzy all day, and with no immunity he can't shake the cold he's caught. In the midst of this, what gives him the most pleasure is the discovery that a pair of white-plumed honeyeaters have built a nest on the back veranda.

They've picked an unlikely spot, the spindly canopy of a potted maple Don had thought was dying. The nest looks so obvious, so vulnerable. The only advantage is it's close to the house and we like birds.

The year before, another pair of honeyeaters—or maybe even this same pair—had nested in a nearby tree. During a storm they were driven away by mynas, so now Don goes outside and shoos away any blackbirds or other introduced species that come too close. He tries to keep Gabriel from banging a plastic hammer within a few metres of the nest, so the pair aren't disturbed from their eggs. When a ball you've kicked lands on the veranda, narrowly missing the maple, he warns you to be more careful: 'If you knock the nest over, you'll regret it for your whole life.'

*Your whole life.*

The month after Gabriel turned four, you turned seven and we didn't speculate on how many birthdays, how much of your lives, your father will share with you. Caught between the cancer and the cure, Don can't get a strange chemical taste out of his mouth. The drugs have affected his concentration. He's finding it hard to work, and one night I ask if he'll instead consider writing down some thoughts for you and your brother.

In dignity therapy, the hospice biographers ask the terminally ill a set of questions meant to refine their sense of life's meaning:

What gave you the greatest sense of accomplishment?
When did you feel most alive?
What have you learned about life that you want
to pass on to others?
What advice or words of guidance would you wish
to pass along to your [son, daughter, husband,
wife, others]?

It's hard for me to imagine your father answering such well-meaning but earnest questions. I'd take his ripostes, though. I'd take some crappy sayings from a calendar, anything.

Occasionally, people will stop Don on the street. One woman told him she'd pinned a speech of his inside her son's wardrobe door. Someone else carries one in his wallet. Can't Don repurpose one of these? I want a series of Polonius-style rules, some multi-purpose commandments we can reach for and abide by. And I'm scared if he gets sicker he won't be able to write at all ... Your friend's parents, with whom we've been travelling in grim parallel, have accepted the tight limit on their days together. They had been hoping to take a last holiday somewhere sunny, to sit and watch their kids playing in a pool. Then, within a matter of weeks, they found they'd crossed a threshold where travel is no longer possible.

The first time I ask Don to write something, he claims to not be wise enough. The second time, the suggestion makes him bristle. He'll try, he tells me, if he knows for certain he's dying. Otherwise, it's too morbid.

One night I have to take him to hospital.

We're watching television and when the episode finishes, he admits that his cold must have worsened. His temperature has hit the danger point of 38°C.

He's soon shaking violently—

with febrile neutropenia,

we subsequently learn—and we leave the house before my brother pulls up to look after you.

Midnight on a weekend in the emergency ward: police officers in bulletproof vests stand around the water cooler. In every cubicle nearby is a fresh drama.

Don is given antibiotics and a range of tests, while behind the next curtain a mother waits for her son. Midway through treatment for head injuries, he's somehow absconded. She sits by the empty stretcher until a man with his forehead bandaged returns, carrying a shopping bag with a six-pack. Risk and damage chasing each other.

When I visit your father the next morning, he's no longer shaking.

I've bought him some travel guides to foreign countries: hope bound in book form.

He looks at them, pleased, then asks for word about the honeyeaters. When he needs to stay in hospital longer, he asks again the next day, and the next.

Now I have to take a more serious interest in them too.

These darting birds have silvery bodies and yellow-green heads. If I catch one's profile, a white neck plume gives the impression it's wearing a pearl necklace, but they move so quickly that between blinks they disappear. I read on a birding website that

their call—*chick-ick-o-wee* or *chirrapo-we-weet*—
is one of the first to be heard in the morning
and the last at night.

It's the female that's built the nest, and
when surreptitiously I approach it to look at her
handiwork I see within the weaving dental floss, string
and hair. It appears to be *my* hair. This Rumpelstiltskin bird has picked threads from our detritus
and spun them into treasure. To finish, the nest has
been bound with spiderweb.

Prior to the nest-building, the male would have performed an
acrobatic courting song: 'male white-plumed honeyeaters', claims
backyardbirds.com, 'make several "song flights" throughout the
day above the treetops while singing a special song, diving steeply
into nearby trees'.

When I first met your father, I was seeing someone else, who
I imagined I would marry.

'Does he make you laugh?' Don asked one day, and my hesita-
tion was the endnote of that other relationship. *His* courting song
included humour. What a quick, original mind. Rare thoughts
came out of it. Like the plants he later chose for the surprises they
offered, he could make words do more than one thing.

He took me out wandering with him. In the bush, picking
our way through bracken, his arm around my shoulder, it became
hard to imagine not having his arm there.

Then once we were driving down a country road when an
old homestead rose up, a Victorian mansion surrounded by

tall trees. We stopped the car and walked towards the mirage, a colonial mirage. The windows were boarded up but the place was not in bad repair. Signs remained of the owner's eccentric attempts at refinement: a pattern painted on the veranda's wooden floor resembling the tiles fashionable in the era, intricately carved woodwork in the style of wrought-iron lace around the veranda posts and balcony. It felt as if the hope of whoever had done this hadn't entirely worn off, even if that hope was blind. And we had the sense that these touches had been put there specifically for us, in this late afternoon, with not another soul around. Walking to the back of the house, we found an old orchard, planted perhaps a century earlier; and within the orchard stood a clutch of quince trees, laden with golden fruit. We picked as much as we could carry in our shirts, turned up to make pouches, before returning to the car.

You were born during an electrical storm, wired and quick and avid, your face balled, Don thought, like Edward G. Robinson's in a noir epic, ready for a fight. Your father and I had lived separately almost until this moment, then set up a house together in haste, in chaos. When your brother came, even as he was swaddled in a baby blanket, he showed his gentle watchfulness—eyes locking on mine—and then in the months to follow, his humour. As a tiny baby, he startled us by letting out peals of high laughter. I hadn't known an infant could laugh like that, as though in on a grand and hilariously absurd joke.

Your father had lived the majority of his life before he and I even met. There are chapters of his history of which I know little. (And I've been grateful too for the past peeling off, the mistakes weighing less.) At a four-year-old's birthday party, the child's grandmother told me she knew Don many years ago, perhaps quite well, through, let's say, Joe Blow.

'I've never heard him mention Mr Blow,' I admitted.

'Well, Don did his eulogy!' she admonished.

Don does everyone's eulogies, I thought and didn't say.

Perhaps that's why he's left instructions with a lawyer that at his own funeral no one is to give a speech.

———

When your father comes home from the hospital he sits on the veranda watching the honeyeaters' nest. Unshaven, thinner, he's staggered, he says, and moved, by all the effort of these small creatures in finding a mate and building a home to raise their young.

I remember he has written before about his love of birds, quoting the poet e.e. cummings:

*may my heart always be open to little*
*birds who are the secrets of living*
*whatever they sing is better than to know*
*and if men should not hear them men are old*

Your friend comes over to play and Don recommends you both stand beside the maple tree. 'Don't speak,' he tells you. 'Be very quiet.'

Above your heads is a grapevine-covered pergola: you're under that pure green of new leaves. Listening, at first there's only the faintest *cheep* from the nest, but it builds and delight spreads over your faces. Your friend, who lives in an apartment building, tells you how lucky you are to have a nest in your garden. To inner-city children, this is no less than magic, and in the days to follow, the wonder's volume rises. *More, more, more!* comes the trill.

The eggs now hatched, the pair of honeyeaters dart around the garden, an olive-tinted shimmer flitting in and out of branches, finding nectar and insects. They're frantic in the way we were when you were newborns. Honeyeaters live in groups, and this pair seem to have relatives nearby; aunts and uncles swoop past to see the babies.

We watch them visit as we go about our business, feeding our own young. At breakfast, you two squabble over the chair that gives a better view of the birds' furious activity.

The greatest tension between Don and me has been over where to live. He would do anything to move us out of the city. He wishes his sons had a chance at the same expansive relationship with nature he had. And on some of these days when he is too ill to work, he ranges around our house like a captive, as if living here, denatured, is what has made him sick.

He loves elements of his garden, but the version of the outdoors he wants you and your brother to enjoy is the one you know best through books. Here nature plays an extensive number of roles: Instructor, Healer, Inspirational Mentor, Bestower of Physical and Moral Health, General Beguiler. Gardens and meadows and woodlands are where children slip the control of adults. They're places kids get to be alone, and experience enchantment, much as the reader does with the book itself.

For Louisa May Alcott, wilderness provided respite from bitter poverty. Her father, Bronson Alcott, was at the centre of the nineteenth-century transcendentalist movement, an offshoot of European romanticism. But his desire to establish a commune near Concord, Massachusetts, free from the taint of commerce, had forced his wife and daughters into a life of deprivation. Louisa bridled at the severity of his idealism, while nevertheless enjoying the company of her father's friends, who were the era's most significant environmental philosophers. The young writer had free reign in Ralph Waldo Emerson's library, and was given natural history lessons by none other than Henry David Thoreau.

Thoreau had stepped back from his family's pencil business to immerse himself in the world outdoors. 'I went to the woods,' he famously wrote in *Walden* (1854), 'because I wished to live deliberately, to front only the essential facts of life, and see if I could not learn what it had to teach, and not, when I came to die, discover that I had not lived.'

Versions of Thoreau, and also Emerson, turn up repeatedly as the male heroes in Alcott's books, including *Little Women*. Alcott rowed with Thoreau across Walden Pond. She and her sisters rambled with him in the woods, hearing about the birds and trees—a cobweb, he told her, was a fairy's dropped handkerchief. Alcott was a witness to Thoreau's all-consuming ecological project and would have known about, and perhaps seen, his scrupulously detailed journals containing observations of the natural world (amounting, in twenty-seven years, to two million words). In this milieu, nature gave Alcott an experience of the godly, which she framed as beneficially familial: 'a vital sense of His presence, tender and sustaining as a father's arms'.

In Frances Hodgson Burnett's memoir, *The One I Knew the Best of All,* she recalled her 1865 emigration from Manchester to Tennessee. Her widowed mother had sought the financial protection of Burnett's uncle, whose American business then soon failed. In the midst of consecutive losses, Burnett described her 'instinct of kinship' with the mountains. She would lie down in a bower of green, 'so quiet that the little living things actually became accustomed ... and quite unafraid'. Birds 'practised their scales just as if she had been one of the family'. Burnett, referring to herself in the third person, claims to have never felt 'quite sober when she lay full length on the grass and pine-needles on a Summer day and closed her eyes'. The experience was one of 'intoxication': she 'was exquisitely happy and uplifted by a strange, still joy—better than anything else in life'.

Lucy Maud Montgomery, who had most likely read both Alcott and Burnett, often detailed the solace of nature in her Anne books ('"Dear old world," she murmured, "you are very lovely, and I am glad to be alive in you."') Reflecting on her own childhood, Montgomery described rambling through the woods of Canada's remote Prince Edward Island in the 1870s and '80s, where she constructed a fantasy of a whole, mended family. Aged twelve, she learnt of her widowed father's remarriage and set off collecting tokens for her new stepmother: 'It gave me exquisite joy to search … until I found something I deemed perfect enough to offer her and I fondly supposed that she would feel on receiving it the same joy I had felt in sending it.' Her pressed ferns, accompanied by 'affectionate letters wherein I poured out my childish soul', went unreciprocated. However, in the woods, Montgomery began to have an experience she named 'the flash'—a sense of ecstatic interconnection with nature. In the midst of a loveless upbringing with strict grandparents, these feelings 'made me love my home because of … the halo they threw over what was otherwise bare and savorless'.

In Europe, as in North America, this preoccupation with the spiritual benefits of being in wilderness flourished alongside the rise of industrialisation, and as more city-dwelling children achieved literacy, a set diet of classics emerged, with 'child' inevitably linked to 'nature'.

Kenneth Grahame, in *The Wind in the Willows*, was 'lamenting the changing environment around him which, with railroad, motor car and urbanisation, seemed to take him further from the idealised haven of his childhood', Jackie Wullschläger notes. For the orphaned Grahame, shunted to his grandmother's crumbling Berkshire mansion, his time outdoors in the freedom of his imagination marked a 'golden age'. It was these landscapes of his childhood to which he remained attached: 'the rambles along dusty lanes and through yellow cornfields' and 'the "stripling Thames" remote and dragonfly haunted'. Grahame has animals—creatures, along with children, of lower status—appreciate this beauty. The sight of the river captivates Mole: 'All was a-shake and a-shiver—glints and gleams and sparkles, rustle and swirl, chatter and bubble', and he feels 'a great Awe upon him'.

Grahame's contemporary, Beatrix Potter, was over the border from him each summer, in the Scottish lowlands, becoming expert in fields as diverse as fossils, fungi and entomology. She later claimed, 'I remember every stone, every tree, the scent of the heather, the music sweetest mortal ears can hear, the murmuring of the wind through the fir trees'. And as she began sketching her own pet rabbit, a family tree emerged in British children's literature, all with a naturalist bent.

J.R.R. Tolkien and C.S. Lewis both admired Kenneth Grahame and Beatrix Potter. For Lewis, Potter's tales were 'the delight of my childhood', and after his mother's death, he and his brother lost themselves in an imaginary saga they devised called 'Animal-Land'. 'The idea of humanised animals fascinated me perhaps even more than it fascinates most children,' he wrote. Tolkien, ten years old when *The Tale of Peter Rabbit* was first published, in 1902, later admired the moral element of the story as a miniature version of *Paradise Lost*. It was *The Wind in the Willows*, however, which claimed his imagination, and *The Hobbit* often reveals the inheritance.

Landscape and loss were as tied together for Tolkien as they had been for Grahame. His life in the northern town of Sarehole, drawing trees and bilberry picking, had been one of great contentment. Humphrey Carpenter, in *J.R.R. Tolkien: A Biography*, writes: 'And because it was the loss of his mother that had taken him away from all these things, he came to associate them with her. His feelings towards the rural landscape became emotionally charged with personal bereavement.'

Coming just after Tolkien and Lewis, Roald Dahl was also of a generation actively encouraged to explore the natural world. His letters home from boarding school detail the respite he found in the Derbyshire land- scape, and in *Danny, the Champion of the World* he describes the moving experience of a child visiting a forest: 'I had a queer feeling that the whole wood was listening with me, the trees and the bushes, the little animals hiding in the under- growth and the birds roosting in the branches. All were listening. Even the silence was listening. Silence was listening to silence.'

It's beautiful, isn't it?

But reading this now, when ecologically the world is going to shit, it has a different valence. There's something mournful, something pitiful about the animals' vigilance. And each book recording it is another piece of a cut-down tree. What, at the rate we're going, will be left of our forests when you come of age?

A 'vital sense', 'a strange, still joy', 'the flash' or 'halo', 'a great awe': these are our children's writers' almost religious descriptions of the outdoors—the sublime trapped in literary amber. But the problem with the romantic tradition exalting God in nature is that, as the philosopher John Passmore wrote, 'It dangerously underesti- mates the fragility of so many natural processes and relationships.'

In our home, in your bedroom, grit sweeps in from the main roads hemming our neighbourhood, leaving a black line along the windowsill and dust on every knick-knack. The nearest natural space is a creek, and every time it rains, the rising water level causes the trees on the banks to bloom with colourful plastic bags.

If these do prove to be your father's last days, even the honey-eaters will remind him of the birds he won't see again. This meagre pot plant is hardly the forest he craves, and each room is cluttered with plastic crap, a piece of Lego always underfoot. Everywhere there are miniature plastic tools and play kitchenware. (The toy oven from IKEA, littered with toy cups and saucers and pretend fruit and chunks of meat, is a send-up; kids mock their parents as much as mimic them.)

While Don's confined with this hoard of modern junk, I try, in fulfilment of some silent promise to him, to find books that cast you into the kind of eco-reveries I imagine he recalls. At present your whole bookshelf is a shrine to anthropomorphism, or 'critter lit' as Ursula K. Le Guin called it. Tigers come to tea, elephants learn to swim at the local pool, hippos yearn to dance. These creatures are friends with chickens and mice and pigs (or at least they're all civil, dropping their offspring at the same child-care centre). The menageries—usually a curation limited to big-eyed animals we regard as cute—visit museums, borrow from the library, host dress-up parties, and even fly overseas, assisting each other with their seatbelts. As we eliminate the planet's wild creatures, we domesticate them in storybooks.

Of course, judging by Aboriginal Australian storytelling, or the ancient Indian *Panchatantra*—or the more recent fables attributed to Aesop two thousand years ago—people have been using animals to instruct children in morals since time before record. It's just ironic that the last thing the stories train kids about is the animals themselves.

In most of your books, a creature is used as a cuddly proxy for teaching human behaviour. So many nights, I've read to you about some rabbit or other being lovingly tucked into bed, while the rabbits introduced by Australian colonists to 'provide a touch of home' have spread faster—as many as twelve in a litter and on their own from three weeks—than any mammal anywhere, decimating indigenous plants and, as a result, animal species. The erosion they've caused on this continent will take centuries to restore. Rather than a connection being built to the natural world through these storybooks, it is severed.

By denaturing these animals, we denature ourselves. Or is it that we're already denatured and so do the same to them?

# Ten

I'm in the kitchen when I register in the maple tree a large black shape. It has a long, sharp beak with a hooked tip. An implacable yellow-eyed gaze. Jet feathers on a short-legged body.

This currawong—named for its onomatopoeic cry—looks ridiculous in such a small plant. The honeyeaters and their relatives are dive-bombing the intruder and it just sits there, hovering over the week-old nestlings. It's barely perturbed, while I let out a scream so guttural and loud it terrifies you two boys and your father, all finishing dinner.

I burst out the back door and the currawong flies to the end of the garden, coming to rest on the high net of the trampoline. Leaning down, I pick up a stone.

'No!' Don, having joined me, places his hand on my wrist to stop me.

He picks up the stone himself, hurling it in the currawong's direction. The bird, seeming to glare, flies off in its clumsy style.

'Get away, you bloomin' bird!' I hear you cry, while Gabriel holds out his small hand to high-five Don.

All four of us are suddenly united against a threat we can see.

By nesting so close to our back door, the honeyeaters were, we'd thought, counterintuitively in a clever, protected spot. It's more likely, however, that the currawong had long been aware of the nest's location and was letting the diligent parents fatten up its dinner. (Each season, Don reads on his phone, currawongs eat forty nests' worth of baby birds to feed their own young.)

Don checks the nestlings. They are still there, blind and weak-necked, their pin or blood feathers just erupting. Their parents, though, are nowhere to be seen.

He hovers in the kitchen, putting things away, wiping down the countertops, the stove. Really he's waiting for the pair to return, and he keeps glancing back at the nest.

His face is whiskery—it hurts too much to shave—and his expression suggests he's thinking that the true horror is not the parents losing their babies, but the reverse.

'There he is, or there she is,' he says suddenly, relieved.

A honeyeater is leaning into the nest, distributing fare.

'Do you think they realise we're trying to protect them?' I know it's a stupid question and yet I don't know.

'I doubt it,' Don answers. 'But I'm grateful they're here.'

'Why?'

He looks at me, embarrassed to say.

Most inner-city gardens are home to introduced species—pigeons, blackbirds, mynas—and he admits that it feels an honour to have the honeyeaters choose to nest here in ours. The birds are a delegation of avian friends. In the midst of his strife their appearance seems a blessing.

Affection for small birds was matrilineal in your father's family. To create their farms, both Don's grandfathers cleared the ancient forest, home of lyrebirds, from their newly acquired blocks of land. Whatever his grandmothers' thoughts were about this horror, they made gardens around their new houses, where, Don has written, 'a few of the native birds went on singing, as if in denial'. Then: 'the little birds came and dwelt in the hydrangeas under the window. Fantails, wagtails, blue wrens, shrub-wrens, honeyeaters, eastern rosella, finches, silvereyes, robins, thornbills, mudlarks and thrushes.' Native birds known to the settlers by these plain English names.

'In the daily contest with nature the women were as determined as the men, as faithful to the cause,' he's remembered in his book *The Bush*. However, they 'made exceptions of the surviving birds. They talked to them, treated them in the garden as companions and friends; saw in them, possibly, intimations of grace. Their sweet and friendly calls, their balletic nectar-sipping sensuality, their brilliance, were hints of another, dreamed about dimension … it was the women's greatest pleasure to make their gardens borders between those two worlds—theirs, the world as it was; and the birds', the world as it had been, before the Fall.'

*Our* garden is now the world before a Fall, a place sectioned off from suffering, but with the currawong about and the light starting to fade, I don't want to leave the nest unattended.

I ask if we should hang sheets on the washing line to block the currawong's view.

Don thinks it will give the honeyeaters a blind side. He imagines covering the area in a net, the gaps only big enough for small birds to travel through.

Sitting by the back door, reading Gabriel a bedtime story, I keep glancing at the nest.

'Stop looking at the birds!' he commands whenever I lose the thread.

Night has fallen and I can see the two of us reflected in the glass—an image of siege.

In a few days, Don will start chemotherapy again. He'll pass hours in the infusion room's high grey vinyl chair, his feet dangling as if he's floating on his own storm cloud. There'll be the rattling of paperwork as his full name and date of birth is double-checked, then the administration of bags containing what is essentially poison.

It seems vital that the birds remain safe.

The next morning, we change our plans and take turns keeping vigil. I work at the kitchen table, and after my parents pick you up from school, they too do a shift as guards. Don feels just well enough to visit friends for dinner, a last supper before the treatment, and I implore the babysitter to watch the nest more closely than you boys.

A little way from the glass doors, she stretches blankets over various pieces of furniture, and we aren't allowed to take this fort-like cubby apart for days. Every cushion in the house pads the cocoon inside, and you are both particularly pleased by the way the seat of the couch now functions as a bookshelf. Here, you've stashed picture books about the everyday dramas of various animals …

… and the story has extended so that we're living within the pages. We're in a children's tale about a human family invested in a honeyeater family.

Beyond our garden is a view of the back street's powerlines. Pigeons sit on the wire as other birds call from nearby gardens. They could all be scouts, members of a resistance banding together to help our heroes live. A beret-wearing sparrow might saunter past with breadstick crumbs and a note in code. See! I can't get outside the conventions of the story, the standard anthropomorphising of animals.

How does this look from the honeyeaters' point of view?

The spine of the bird and the spine of the maple leaf are the same size. The leaf, another object in an enlarged world, is saturated in ultraviolent pigments humans can't see. The honeyeaters live in a nectar-coloured sphere. Those jet eyes on the sides of their yellow heads give them a 300-degree field of vision, meaning they can spy sugar in the rich hues all around them—even while in the air, experiencing their bodies as part of a magnetic field, even while navigating constant threat.

What if children's books do capture an essential truth about animals—that their emotional lives are as rich as ours?

Scientists and animal behaviouralists have shown that birds' days *are* full of versions of love and pride and frustration and fear and sorrow. So again, what is this tale from the bird's point of view?

Their plotline is that of a thriller.

The birds race to find enough hours to ensure their family's safety. Some bird form of anxiety and hope commingling, as the best and worst endings stretch forward. The honey-eaters' tiny hearts keeping rapid time: da-DUM-da-DUM da-DUM-da-DUM da-DUM-da-DUM da-DUM-da-DUM da-DUM-da-DUM da-DUM-da-DUM da-DUM-da-DUM da-DUM-da-DUM da-DUM-da-DUM da-DUM-da-DUM da-DUM-da-DUM da-DUM-da-DUM da-DUM-da-DUM da-DUM-da-DUM da-DUM-da-DUM da-DUM-da-DUM da-DUM.

When the person you love could be dying, it's as if the curtains are coming down on the whole world. And indeed, daily the news confirms this to be the case—the planet's trees and rivers and creatures *are* dying. What to do with this grief? The easy-to-ignore horror of living through a mass extinction? If we want nature to be of solace to children in times of strife—and

I do want you to learn from nature's cycles—we need to be frank about how humans have disrupted these cycles. And increasingly, to find ways to talk about all that is being lost.

Later, in a dedicated children's bookshop near our house, I notice the proliferating array of environmental children's titles: *Planet SOS; You Can Change the World; Old Enough to Save the Planet; Our House is On Fire; Kids Fight Plastic; My Friend Earth; Greta's Story: The Schoolgirl Who Went on Strike to Save the Planet.* One way to produce a different future is to imagine a different future. Perhaps the unbridled creativity we celebrate in children's literature will loosen an idea in a future scientist or activist that saves us. But it's a head-spinning graduation: kids move from a lulling diet of Peter Rabbit spin-offs to being required to fix climate change. Instead of turning off the bedside light, basking in fantasy, no one can sleep.

—

We keep the vigil going for a few days, but it becomes clear we can't surveil the nest full-time. While you're at school, I take Gabriel to visit the zoo. We wander around with the other families who are dealing with life and death, gazing into enclosures where all the animals are doing the same. Then we get back in the car and drive home.

As I turn the front door key, he offers this risk assessment: 'Everyone won't die this minute.'

'No,' I agree. 'They won't.'

'It's not dying
season,' he explains breezily, walking past me inside.

He's wrong, though: the next morning your friend's mother
sends through a text message that his father has died. She was
holding his hand. Their children were by his side.

It's a grey spring day, dismal even before this news, and
outside the weather turns steadily worse. Rain lashes down all
afternoon. Your sister delivers Don home from the hospital, and
I tell him what's happened.

He can't speak. Silently he goes outside and when eventually
he returns, I realise he's been checking on the birds. 'There's only
one in the nest now,' he says. 'The wind has blown the others
out—that, or the nest's been raided.'

Neither of us thinks at the time of the symbolism.

'Could the birds have flown away?'

'We can imagine that.'

He hasn't seen any fledglings on the nearby ground, and he's
unsure whether the parents will keep feeding the one that's left.

I creep outside and, standing on a bench, spy a ball of feathers. The ball isn't moving.

The garden beyond seems soggy and wonder-less.

A ridiculous fantasy has suddenly been revealed. In children's books, the garden is a place only of freshness, of greenness. A place of healing where the lame learn to walk again, and the lonely find their kin. Becoming more conscious of our garden, noticing that the air is perfumed with rosemary and jonquils, and actually stopping and *looking* at the plants, really looking, was I willing a similar kind of enchantment? Did I think that by some feat of imagination, we could switch our story's genre, and change its ending? Would I squint and find fairies taking tea under the violets?

Even more shameful, there's a convention in these kinds of tales in which a human helps an animal—removing a thorn from a paw, or easing hunger with a morsel—that has the animal repaying the act with its ongoing loyalty and protection. Did I think our family's efforts to save the baby honeyeaters should be repaid by nature treating us and our friends in ways that are solely benign; that is to say, by everyone staying alive?

Later, Don and I tell you boys about your friend's father.

'Really?' you say over and over, as though we might be joking. 'Really?'

Gabriel just keeps playing with Lego, and before long, that's what you are doing too. It's disconcerting how unmoved you both seem, how little comment this has provoked. I could have mentioned we were low on milk for all the effect the news has had.

When my brother arrives for dinner, you and Gabriel invite him inside the cubby, and you show your uncle the books on your couch-shelf. Don has retreated to bed, while I bang around saucepans, trying to cook. The news is on in the background, and I wonder how to defend you against stagnant wages, artificial intelligence, climate-change-driven wars, the liberal world order collapsing, in time for you to fledge.

'I want to tell you a story,' I hear you tell your uncle tentatively. 'It's about my friend's dad … He died of cancer.'

*I want to tell you a story …*

The form of this! All the time I'd been devising how best to give you information, when you already knew. A story is the vehicle for difficult truths, for news you may still be trying to understand yourself. Which kind of story? Any kind, as long as its form is condensed and resonant. No grand tricks, no showing off. C.S. Lewis liked the genre's restraint, the 'strict limit on vocabulary'. (Although *The Cat in the Hat* took a year to write. The three hundred and thirty-eight words in *Where the Wild Things Are* took two years.) The best work, you might agree, doesn't dress up the banal as profound, or tell children things out of convenience, to spare adults having to think harder. E.B. White feared that, writing for young readers, he'd 'slip into a cheap sort of whimsy or cuteness … I don't trust myself in this treacherous field,' he admitted, 'unless I am running a degree of fever.' The right story can also break a fever. You've probably gathered that adults read these books aloud not only to soothe children.

Sitting at the table, eating dinner with you two boys and my sibling—my parents also now so often in and out of the house—I have to work hard to keep the lines of who's an adult and who's a child from blurring. This isn't a problem for the honeyeaters. Miraculously, I see them returning, and after their absence they work manically to feed the remaining nestling. Often both give food to the baby at once, lavishing it with care—except there's not just one baby. Three yellow beaks shoot straight up when their parents hover overhead. In the five or so days since the currawong's visit their necks have strengthened, and now they crane in synch to get their due. This is the second time they've surprised us.

Had Don only imagined the birds gone in his moment of grief?

He's devastated for your friend and his sister and mother— and he himself has lost a comrade. Our neighbourhood feels full of fit young dads jogging and kicking and cycling with their kids, their ubiquity almost a parody. At school functions, the two ill men were drawn together, relieved, perhaps, to find, amidst all the sturdy fathers with children slung easily over their shoulders, another person who truly understood.

Out the window, the birds work with renewed urgency. One parent does the feeding, while the other makes repairs to the strained nest. The intensity of this cycle—the fear, the hope, the devoted exuberance of their parenting. The dying man's last breath, a deep one, I hear later, was inhaling his son and daughter.

———

Your friend comes over while his mother organises the memorial service. He visits Don, lying curled and thin, in the spare room. Taking in a harmonica, he blows the sick father a tune, maybe a charm to raise him out of bed. When it's time to play 'schools', he returns to Don and tries to cajole him into getting up.

'You can be one of the students,' he promises.

Don has to apologise: he just doesn't feel able.

Both you and Gabriel are more pliable, as if you've previously agreed your friend should decide the game and everyone's role within it. Gabriel is given an array of bit parts. It can seem you and your friend are doing him a favour, allowing him to play, whereas it's an act of generosity him allowing himself to be directed, or ordered, through various scenes. Scenes where you two express the swampy feelings about one father having so far been granted a reprieve.

When I drive your friend home, you both sit in the backseat discussing the books you want to read next. (The day he returned to school, you took along a volume on predatory animals to cheer him up.)

'I really want a copy of *Wild Animals of the South*,' you admit.

'Why don't you ask Father Christmas to bring it?' he advises. 'That way you'll save your mum the money.'

The songs of innocence and experience play over each other.

———

His dad loved football and so the service is held at the local club. In front of the goalposts, the old grandstand's tiered seating is full. You give me the slip and barge through the crowd to sit in the front row next to your friend. Both of you listen to the celebrant for a while, before wriggling out of your seats to get onto the grass. Now mourners have a view of those giving speeches, and also, past them, children playing football on the green oval.

Time is altered at the edges of a death: the deceased is still here and not here. He's very present, and yet how quickly the conjugations of the verbs change. There's a brutality even to our grammar. It is jarring hearing the celebrant move straight to the past tense: *was*, not *is*.

Before we've all refiled the missing person from ALIVE to DEAD, a chasm opens up. One we could all fall into.

On the bright field, a blur of young children run and stretch and kick the ball—a ballet of chaos and will.

While running, even in full view, your friend and his sister have privacy. It doesn't matter that they haven't learnt the small talk the bereaved need to master, the polite ways to bat back *I'm so sorry* and *If there's anything I can do*. Adults may look at them with sad expressions as if to say, You don't yet understand—but what is there to understand? The lost person is only days gone. He could open the front door at any moment and walk back inside. Why should this not be some passing incident—as every other episodic part of life has so far been?

———

Soon after Don's diagnosis, I read an essay by the children's literature historian Francelia Butler, in which she noted that a famous six-volume catalogue of folk literature 'abounds with references to restoration of life, either by magical re-assemblage of the body's dispersed members, or by administration of the water or life, or by medicines, or in various other ways'. In these stories, she adds:

> Men may come back as women or women as men. People may become children, dwarves, monsters, princes or princesses, stars or angels or gods. They can return to earth as fish, horse's heads, donkeys, cows, bulls, oxen, calves, buffalo, swine …

When I first started reading this list, I was infuriated. How could *anyone* comfort a child with these tales? The thought of a loved one returning as a swine hardly sold reincarnation. How many more unanswerable questions would you inevitably serve up to me on hearing this? And yet as the list continued, it had a mesmerising quality, like an incantation summoning

wild boar, goats,

cats, dogs,

lions, wolves,

rabbits, foxes, deer,

seals, bears, hyenas,

jackals, elephants,

monkeys, rats, otters,

ducks, owls, hawks,

eagles, swallows, cuckoos,

doves, pigeons, ravens,

quails,

partridges,

herons, cranes,

geese, peacocks,

parrots, snakes, lizards,

crocodiles, tortoises,

or frogs.


Or they may come back as bees,

butterflies, fleas, weevils, bedbugs,

salmon, goldfish, sharks, whales,

leeches, scorpions, crabs.


Again, they may turn into trees,

roses, lilies, lotus,

grass, straw, herbs,

bramble-bushes, tobacco plants,

peanut plants, eggplants,

musical instruments,

dishes, fountains,

balls,

wind,

stones,

salt,

smoke …

Now I can accept the point.

The seeds of these stories are countless years old, and for millennia we've been seeing our lost loved ones in enchanted and haunted places all around us. Life ends, but not entirely. Our missing person *does* live on in eggplants, musical instruments, fountains; that is to say, in the memories we attach to food or songs or gardens. The lost one becomes internalised: they're someone with whom we have a different, private relationship. But for those at the start of life, how to comprehend that each day will stretch on, and lead to more days with the irreplaceable person gone?

In class, you're being taught to tell the time. I find you drawing circles and filling them with clock faces. It's another thing to have to learn that time can be forever.

# Eleven

Those on the quest grow weary. Often, they've forged through many different landscapes—dense forest with bifurcating trees, mountains of sand, swamps concealing unknown perils. The changing vistas present new tests, each one more difficult than the previous, until slowly it dawns on these heroes that the greatest challenge, the journey to the underworld, still lies before them.

Inevitably, they wonder if they'll survive—they're wrestling with an unforgiving geography and their own volatile internal landscape. Doubt, fatigue, frustration and rage at the toll of accumulating losses meant Odysseus's 'spirit was crushed by the sea'. But he 'sailed on; grieved at heart, glad to have escaped death', while thinking of his 'dear comrades'. When eventually he and his crew found a harbour, they pulled in unable to speak, 'and lay there for two days and two nights, eating our hearts for weariness and sorrow'.

Our household tries to steer away from strong emotions. Out-bursts use too much energy. Each of us is instead learning the art of suspension. It involves not thinking past each day; any further and panic can rise. There's such a distance to fall so it's best not to look too far ahead or down. All we know are the parameters set for each 24-hour block. 'What's happening tomorrow?' you ask at night as I turn out the light. That's the future, only that. We adjust to the sway of the rope, trying to stay steady as we move between the house and the hospital and the school. After pick-up and dinner, the last stretch of the day includes the school-sanctioned twenty minutes of reading practice.

One night, you produce a reader titled *In Search of the Mummy*, and, sitting in the kitchen between your father and Gabriel, you open the first page. '"The ancient Egyptians lived a long time ago in Africa ..."'

You now read well, better than either of us can remember reading at the same age. In the midst of turmoil has come this expansion.

'"We know a lot about them because they made amazing graves called tombs. The ancient Egyptians made these tombs because they believed that when you died, you began a new life—an afterlife."'

Don sees a chance: 'A lot of people believe in an afterlife.'

It's the first time I've heard him talk about this—the first time he's acknowledged he needs to. Even if he believes we meet with extinction, he doesn't mind you having some mythology to deal with death.

Gabriel has drifted away; he'd rather a story than a lesson. But you listen to your father, taking in the words he's saying and not saying, before returning to the book.

Over the clatter of my dishwasher stacking, I can hear you reading about princes being buried with lavish food and inlaid board games. I'm distracted, though: my domestic skills haven't suddenly improved in the light of our circumstances. The kitchen had always been Don's domain. It takes me ages to do things he knocked over quickly.

You start outlining the preservation of the well-heeled dead: 'all the squishy parts or organs were taken out while the heart was left … The stomach, intestines, liver and lungs are washed in a special salt … Then the organs are put in jars … a different jar for each organ … The body was filled with sawdust, leaves, linen and sweet-smelling spices.'

I glance over at your father, who's already nauseous from the drugs. He's leaning forward, his head in his hands.

I move to take his place and wordlessly he returns to bed.

The page is open to an image of a brown, wrinkled *thing*. It's strangely human and not. A mahogany branch with high cheek-bones, pronounced shoulders, and hips growing stick-like arms and legs. It's a photograph of a mummified figure, stripped of the bandages.

Should you even be reading this? It both demystifies and re-mystifies death. Is it good for us to be talking about these subjects that can make a stomach lurch? Or was it insensitive of me not to have foreseen what could happen in this situation?

Recently, Don has confessed he feels different suddenly. *Very* not right. He fears that the chemicals pumped through his body have triggered some further problem, that his last years with you will be spent like this, fighting for extra life while feeling he's already partially mummified.

'Priests sang special chants,' you continue, 'for each part of the body, even the fingers and toes.'

The day before, to keep the house quiet, I'd drawn around your toes. You and your brother lay on a sheet of butcher's paper as I traced your outlines, working the pen around your heels and the sides of your feet, noticing the toenails I needed to clip. Not too long ago, I knew every inch of your bodies—the impunity of touching that perfect flesh! I still have the sense that your flesh is connected to mine. *I made these toes; I grew them.* But in the tracing, it was clear how much you're both loosening out of the baby fat and emerging as tall, thin creatures. Flashes of who you'll both be are in your gangliness, your smiles; and down on the floor, you set to work, filling in your bodies' outlines with glowing texta colour.

Now your book moves past mummified animals—a cat, a crocodile, an ibis, a baboon—to tomb design. Boxes within boxes, in rooms within rooms. Tutankhamun's tomb consisted of four golden shrines, arranged one inside the other. The doors of the fourth shrine opened to reveal a stone box. Inside it were three coffins, each smaller than the last, the final one built of gold.

'What if there's not an afterlife?' you turn and ask.

My heart thuds. 'I suppose we can't know for certain.'

'I want to find out.' You say it so darkly, it sounds like a death wish.

'But I don't want you to die!' I blurt out.

Your friend's dad will know if there's an afterlife, you point out.

'Yes.' *I wish so much to be better at this. Be patient, I'll get there.* 'He'll be finding out.'

I gather you and your friend don't discuss the death. When I raise the possibility that you might ask him how he's feeling, you become impatient. Why would you ask? His dad is gone and he's ferociously sad. You don't need him to *tell* you that! You know because he is allowed to read a book in class, while the rest of you sit in a circle. You know because at lunchtime you're fighting over umpiring decisions: who scored a goal, who deserves a free kick, who gets to control a playground game when the rest of life is out of control. And meanwhile, privately both of you wonder about an afterlife.

In a guidebook that early on your friend's mother gave me, there was a passage that stuck in my head. The author, a bereavement specialist from the Midwest of the United States, claimed that while some families had firm cultural or religious beliefs about what followed death, most didn't. Most people she met through her work had no real clue, and the author urged her readers to get one, to work out *now* what they believed. Making a broad claim, she darkly advised: 'At some point your children will ask it: Why? ... All I can do is warn you: It is coming and you must be ready for it. *Why does God make people die?*'

As a boy, your father went to Sunday school and occasionally accompanied his family to church. Any church-going child knows what it's like waiting for that hour to pass. Trying to sit still. A show of pious singing to prove one's paying attention. The surreptitious study of the other parishioners. 'Viewed through a child's eyes,' Don has written of those Presbyterians he gawped at, they 'might have risen from the grave for the occasion; their transparent skin like parchment maps … stretched so tight across their noses and around their mouths it was a wonder they could talk, much less sing hymns.'

*The Lord's my shepherd, I'll not want; /He makes me down to lie. /In pastures green …*

We sang the psalm too, every few weeks, at the girl's school that I attended, twenty or so years later, *I'll not want* reverberating while I tried to work out what was best to un-desire. My parents took us to church intermittently, but the school provided no religious instruction, just a daily Anglican hymn. Did it occur to me or any of my classmates that the pastures green belonged to heaven? It sounded so like where we were already. There was an immaculate green sports field, and walking home each afternoon along the half-asleep streets, I passed one beautifully tended lawn after another. Nothing was out of place. Surfaces were important. What lay underneath, as with the meaning of the song, was generally avoided.

At some point, Don, in the small wooden church in Poowong—the angles of which were so tight his grandmother's coffin barely fit out the door—lost his faith. And singing hymns at school, I suppose the same thing happened to me. (As a thirteen-year-old, I wasn't allowed to attend my grandmother's funeral in case it *upset* me.) And here lies the problem. Both of us, in our different times and places, were raised not to talk about these things. Recognising you're repressed, however, doesn't cure you of the affliction. I envy those who are *more* repressed, and armed with religious stories to comfort their kids. When Don's prognosis was worst, we of course spoke of whether we'd see each other again. Who doesn't secretly or not so secretly wonder this?

One night, I tried out a theory that some trace of the love people share continues to exist. 'Then so must a trace of their hate,' Don said, 'and a never-ending battle of good and evil is too much to bear.' He considered his own lack of faith a burden, but added, 'Imagine living for eternity. The earth's already been going for four and a half billion years. What the fuck would you do?'

I turned then to the bookshelves.

But the book I'd imagined I'd find, the book to settle all your questions and fears, I can't picture anymore. Metaphors about stars and sea can only get you so far: the reality of this death so close to us has made casting it as anything other than painful seem dishonest.

Meanwhile, your questions are resolutely pragmatic. 'When you die does all your skin disappear?'

I'm lying next to you in your dark bedroom—it's after the reading about ancient Egyptians. Your brother's knocked out in the parallel bed, and you're meant to be drifting to sleep too, not picturing our transformation to skeletons.

'No, a body takes a long time to decompose.'

I remind you of a book on our shelf, the beautiful and intricately drawn *Leaf Litter: Exploring the Mysteries of a Hidden World* by Rachel Tonkin, which chronicles a year of change in a forest's undergrowth. ('Leaves teach us how to die,' wrote Thoreau.) A blue-tongue lizard decays, and we see in cross-section the carcass breaking down, its nutrients moving through the soil.

'Do you go cross-eyed?' You've seen cartoons, old *Tom and Jerry* episodes, where the character's eyes become spirals before they keel backwards.

'No, but someone usually closes the dead person's eyelids.'

You don't ask why God makes us need to do this, but your questions reveal the split between our understanding of death's physical and spiritual consequences. The physical questions are easier to deal with, although, of course, they often overlap with the metaphysical.

Once, a few years ago, you were walking through a cemetery with your older sister when you tried to lift the top off a granite sarcophagus. 'How do you get out?' you asked. Then: 'Do they bury your nostrils? Do they bury your breath?' The same questions the ancient Egyptians possibly asked their parents. Children commonly wonder if the recently deceased can breathe underground, whether they are hungry, if they're cold. Researchers suggest that children typically grasp the biological effects of death first, then overlay spiritual beliefs.

Now you ask the hardest question—you want to know if the dead remember us, specifically if your friend's dad will remember him.

The dark feels alive, so who can tell what else might be?

'I don't know.' I say. 'No one knows if the dead remember us, because, again, no one's really sure what happens when we die.'

Lying with you, I try to outline a few popular theories, building on what your father has told you. I explain that some people feel they will become part of the universe, or that they'll go whence they came, to a river or a waterhole on their ancestral homeland. Some people believe they will return as other creatures and live many lives. Some people believe in heaven, as our forebears did, a paradise where they will meet again with all the people they love.

Evidently, I don't make this last option sound convincing.

You become fixated on the idea that everyone in heaven is deceased. 'So, it's a place for dead people to meet up?'

'I suppose so.'

You're incredulous with scorn. 'What do they *do* there? They can't talk. They're dead!'

The next morning you say to me, 'I know how to spell "confused" and "incredible"—c-o-n-f-u ...'

And it turns out you do.

———

In late November, you follow your friend's advice, posting a letter to the North Pole:

Dear Santa, have a good Christmas,
can you please get me: Wild Animals of the South
ps could you please get my brother a book to

At a shopping centre, Gabriel rushes to an ornate Christmas tree. He picks up each gift-wrapped present underneath, and I watch his face recalibrate as he realises they are props, empty.

The tree is made of plastic. Just thinking about the smell of pine needles makes Don feel bilious, so you boys and I are in Kmart, looking to purchase one of these fakes. Tinsel and baubles are made for desperate people—all the scorn I've ever felt for this stuff now evaporates. I want every shiny thing, as if it has proven therapeutic value. Any sparkling item that diverts the eye and heart.

Back at home, instead of pine, our living room reeks of plastic. You've chosen a silver tree with LED lights attached to each branch. We decorate these glittering twigs with iridescent clip-on birds, ornaments that can fit so nicely in a little hand. (This is the first year we can trust the youngest of us to resist taking all these decorations off again.) You've already wrapped some lumpy-shaped presents and we stow them underneath.

Your father comes in and sits at the kitchen table. A shy admirer, he's taking in your excitement from a safe distance. In the worn brown pelt of his dressing gown, his shoulders are hunched. He's turned inwards, with the air of someone concentrating very hard on an impossible equation. He wants to be near you but any noise or disruption throws him. Pain calls again and he departs for somewhere we can't follow.

These days, he isn't venturing into his office or very far into the garden. There's no longer a reprieve mid-cycle in his treatment; each day is worse than the day before, and the oncologist has admitted he doesn't like the escalating side effects. If the cancer cells are at an acceptable level, Don might be allowed a break from the treatment. To check, he's been given another biopsy, and we're waiting on the results. On his already aching body, the needle into the pelvic bone has left him tender. When he moves it's gingerly, 'like an old granny', you notice.

Having hung the last shining bauble on our plug-in tree, you are then ready to turn on the lights. Gabriel demands that Don come closer to witness the tree's metamorphosis. You wait, finger on the switch, then flick it.

The colour scheme of fairytales is bold—silver, gold, red, white, green and black—a palette of treasure, blood, snow, the lustrous woods, a witch's cloak. These shades are all flickering off the tree, filling the room with too much poignancy. Your father's illness has cracked our world open. Some moments it's confusing how vividly we seem to be living.

Living 'in the moment' is a mantra Don has always found ridiculous. 'What if the moment is a terrible one?' he'd ask. 'You're in South Sudan trying to survive drought and starvation with someone shooting at you?' But this moment, this exact moment, is, for us, not so bad. Not knowing the biopsy results may be better than knowing, and the Christmas lights signal that school is about to end for the year, with the promise for you and your brother of a long, warm stretch of freedom ahead. The honeyeaters have fledged, and we're here together, adjusting bird ornaments on our big kitsch branches. 'Early summer days are a jubilee time for birds', wrote E.B. White in his classic on mortality, *Charlotte's Web*. 'In the fields, around the house, in the barn, in the woods, in the swamp—everywhere love and songs and nests and eggs … The song sparrow, who knows how brief and lovely life is, says, "Sweet, sweet, sweet interlude, sweet; sweet, sweet, sweet interlude."'

'The birds are flying!' Gabriel exclaims, staring at the ornaments.

'The birds are flying,' your father slowly repeats.

Glitter is already dropping off the branches and coating the floor in a fine silver powder.

Ignore that, don't look down. Keep staring at the lit tree. Just stay like this, in our own bauble. Never look down.

Under the boat is deep, black water.

This is what my friend tells me about her grief. Grief has pulled her out further than she thought she could go. To the edge of what it is possible to bear, of what's habitable, and then further again. The boat that takes the loved one to the underworld turns those who remain into castaways. Cut adrift, they have to find their own way back to the mortal world, to life. The poet Denise Riley describes the dark travel that mourning requires as being like 'virulent jetlag, but surging up in waves'. My friend tells me it bypasses the head and happens through her body. 'Maybe we have short-circuited,' she says.

This grief, it turns out, scares those who get close to it. Even its scent makes people uncomfortable. 'Too evident sorrow does not inspire pity but repugnance,' wrote the French historian Philippe Ariès, 'it is the sign of mental instability or of bad manners: it is morbid.'

Around my friend's children, other adults are suddenly mired in awkwardness. The survivors of the shipwreck have torn clothes and kelp in their hair. People don't know what to do with their sympathy, or their antipathy, because the bereaved are a reminder of the worst possibility, and therefore an affront to happy families. The grief-stricken have to try to act normally so as not to frighten the school mums and dads and teachers.

Your friend and his sister notice that very quickly no one mentions their father, as though his death were somehow shameful. I'm sure people don't intend to upset these kids, but the loved one is somehow taken away again, erased further.

'One thing you can do,' my friend tells me, 'is to mention their father's name, and ask if they're missing their dad. Or even put it jokingly, "What would Dad say about that?"'

In other words, in the most modest way, keep him alive.

# Twelve

Compared to the frenetic pace that's building outside, the Christmas shoppers in the children's bookstore are ceremonially polite: 'You first.' 'No, you.' All is calm, all is bright, apart from the carnival on the shelves. Rows of picture books, each cover painstakingly designed in new, enticing styles, vie for attention and dollars. Fruit, trucks, rainbows have grown eyes and mouths, springing to life. Animals painted in Aboriginal-dot or Western form are dancing, playing instruments, stargazing, while further into the shop, on the jewel-coloured books for older children, there are compasses, or dragons, or castles. Castles are everywhere. On each shelf is another promised land …

I find the nature section.

*Wild Animals of the South* is not in stock.

There are numerous other anthologies, beautifully illustrated with rare creatures, although, like the other books in the store, they mostly depict the world as adults would prefer it to be. The animals roam pristine jungles and swim in sparkling seas.

My gaze stays locked on the shelves to avoid any conversation. As we get closer to hearing the biopsy's results, I feel stiffer than other people; something cold is flowing through my veins.

The browsers around me negotiate their prams through the maze of shelves. They select Christmas presents, and chat and laugh with the sales assistants wrapping their books; and this performance of weary good cheer by everyone is bracing when it feels like any tiny thing could send us veering towards the existential.

A few days earlier, you and I were driving and you were looking through the windscreen at blue sky accented by cumulus. 'I wish I was a cloud,' you said, 'so I'd never have to die.'

'Even clouds die in their own way, when it rains.' I waited. 'Are you worried about your dad?'

The lightning-quick deflection. 'Are you?'

In the British Museum, I've seen a mummy that was buried with a stone scarab so that the heart couldn't testify against it.

'I'm hopeful,' I answered tightly, 'and I'll stay hopeful until I hear the situation is more serious.'

Your silence was too knowing.

I come to the small selection on bereavement at one end of a shelf. I check it again.

It's not that there's nothing here for us. There is, but they are always the same few picture books.

Wolf Erlbruch's *Duck, Death and the Tulip* opens with a duck which has the feeling it is being followed. Looking over its shoulder, the duck spies a skeletal character: '"Good," said Death, "you finally noticed me."' The Danish writer Glenn Ringtved's *Cry, Heart, But Never Break* tells of a black-cloaked figure visiting a house of children the night their grandmother is to die. The children try to distract the uninvited guest, who finally tells them a story, explaining, 'Who would yearn for day if there was no night?' In *Michael Rosen's Sad Book*, written after the death of his son, Rosen describes trying to appear happy so people will not be repelled by his grief, which is 'a cloud that comes along and covers me up'. In *The Memory Tree*, by Britta Teckentrup, animals in a forest hold a memorial for their friend, a dead fox. As they share their recollections, a beautiful tree grows to give them shelter.

I've bought all these titles and others too.

But the truth is, half this collection is still in my study and I haven't actually read them to you and your brother. Often a book will seem too hot or too cold, too hard or too soft. That or there's a threshold I can't cross. I'm not saying none of the books have helped; they have. When I've best handled your questions, it's been because I've thought of a picture or phrase from one of those stories. They've shown me how to set a tone; they've given an example of framing things in a way that feels simple and true.

There's always a point, though, at which death defies language. For most of us, there's the thing we should have said. The better goodbye that could have been made. The wiser condolence to offer the grieving. Death makes the bystander gauche. The ideal sentence flickers away and what's left is just the weather of loss. There needs to be a book whose pages are only of wind and rain.

But what is not in this shop, or any shop, is *the* story with the magic combination of words to transport you somewhere safe. It turns out instead that everyone has to pick a tale about death that best suits them. We assemble our own paper boats, from old designs or whatever scraps of love and hope are at hand.

After your cloud comment we pulled up outside our house, and you wanted to clarify again that when people die they are buried or burnt. There's a brutality to digesting this news for the first time, and realising it has happened to someone we know.

I started taking you through the mechanics of how we deal with bodies, trying to temper this with the joy-highlighting upside of death, but from my mouth even I heard the sound of platitudes.

As you nodded, eyes forward, I could feel myself, fingers outstretched, groping round in the dark for a happy ending. 'Many people think our souls live on.'

'But this is your sole.' You pointed to your foot.

'Your soul is your essence,' I said, experiencing the relief the first person must have felt when they hit upon this concept, and found it soothed those around them. 'Your soul is supposed to be the most *you* part of you. Even when your body dies the soul is separate. It's said to keep living.'

We both felt better, able to go inside and face the night ahead.

Hearing you—and later Gabriel, when my parents dropped him home—your father got out of bed and stood in the back garden in his pyjamas to join a game of French cricket. You threw the ball and he lifted the bat as a shield against your vigour. He hit the ball. You caught it: hold it, gone, hold it, gone.

*I'd sell my soul,* we commonly say, to explain the depths of a desire. This soul we'd all trade might make a kind of intuitive sense but it is still a human invention, an act of storytelling. And historically, at least in the West, only humans have one, putting us on a different plane to the animals around us.

What I'm trying to say is our favourite bedtime tales concern transcendence.

The bookshop's ceiling is painted black, and fairy lights are strung above us shoppers, making a phosphorescent net, seizing all these kids' books in one haul.

Nearly all these stories on the shelves are about people, be they in boats or on broomsticks, taking impossible journeys. This is *the* story of our species, after all—the story of the first diaspora and all those since, imprinted in one way or another on our brains.

As humans spread out over the globe, crossing seas, through every kind of environment and climate, the hardships of the journey were encoded in tales that were then swapped like currency, and standardised to end in triumph. We *have* as a species traversed the sands, scaled mountains, forged rivers, mapped the depth of the oceans. We've quested everywhere on the planet, and as we've transcended geographic and spacial boundaries, we've also transcended physiological ones. People now constantly evade the land of the dead: advances in science can give years and years more life.

The upside of this quest is that, like the heroes of our oldest tales, we have found the treasure: the gold and precious metals, the oil and coal, the life-saving elixirs. The downside is that wherever we triumphantly arrive, we set about ruining the place.

Sometimes, even as I contort my heart and mind into any shape I can to aid Don's survival, even as I think I'd sell my soul to keep him here, I recognise there's something off-kilter in this attitude. I have the disease that Ged, the wizard-king, rails against in Ursula K. Le Guin's *The Farthest Shore*. He realises that the gap in the land of the dead through which the deceased can escape has led to an 'unmeasured desire for life', tipping the world's balance. 'The Unmaking' is upon them, a time of Earthly destruction where no one remembers the right name for ancient things. Trees have stopped flowering. Rivers run dry. Because people want to live forever the world is dying. Ged must use the last drop of his powers to reseal this hole, for to 'refuse death is to refuse life'. However, he knows the enemy is not the wizard who created the exit, but us, 'the self that cries *I want to live; let the world burn so long as I can live!* The little traitor soul in us, in the dark, like the worm in the apple.'

We'll use science to cure ourselves, but ignore it when the lives of other species are at stake. We'll let everything else die to save our loved ones. And I'm guilty too. Standing in the book-shop, full of indignation and exhaustion, I want to scream: *Let the world burn if my children's father can live!*

Nearby is a stack of kids' books about saving the planet, yet there are many more sea-faring adventures, even as the oceans are filling with plastic. Or tales of enchanted woods, abounding with toffee and fairies, while we keep erasing our forests. We've used monsters as coded imposters for those who are different—including those who think differently about water and trees. We've created ballet-slipper-pink books for girls, and black-covered books about galactic war for boys. And if we don't rewrite the characters and the quest, and make a different ending, the cosmic lights will turn off for all of us.

*Goodnight trees,*
*goodnight seas.*

*Goodnight clean air,*
*farewell species everywhere!*

This will be our real, and final, bedtime story.

TEAR IT
ALL UP

STORIES
    AREN'T HELPING



        TEAR THE PAGES UP ...

THEY'RE ONLY MAKING
THINGS WORSE

NO STORIES,
*NO* MORE

RIP THEM UP
AND START AGAIN!

I'm sorry, I'll calm down …

Give me a moment.

I should have told you that your noticing the clouds demonstrates death's ability to show us beauty. A white mass in a blue sky seems more vivid when we realise we have limited time to see it. Our mortality casts our days as precious, revealing the fantastic in the seemingly mundane. Try to keep looking outwards: those cumulus are filled with billions of ice crystals perfectly shaped to scatter light beams, mixing every colour and delivering the cloud direct to your eyes as white. If we pay attention, Death can show us how best to live. What happens after we die, I don't know. Perhaps we'll discover you were right, and that being a cloud is easier.

# Thirteen

Sometimes we sneak a look at the last page of a book to see if it is safe to read on. We want to find out if the protagonist survives. We don't like not knowing what's going to happen, even though this not-knowing is the tension that keeps us reading. The potential for the good *and* bad ending propels us forward, but I'm unable to turn to the page with your father's biopsy results. Time is measured by the proximity to his appointment with the oncologist. There's a week to go, then a few days, then just twelve hours. And finally I'm driving Don down the same old streets, which now have a layer of portent not readable before.

He's palpably solid, showered and dressed, smelling of soap and coffee, but around us everything feels temporary. Along the flat, straight road into the city, the Victorian buildings make a grubby stage set. FOR LET signs are plastered to windows, paint is peeling. It's all a façade and ready to suddenly be switched off, leaving just the screen of overcast sky, the intricate churning of clouds.

Closer to the city centre, the buildings give way to restaurants and shops. There are more and more people in the streets, and they move around so blithely. In their collective nonchalance they seem to be from a different world. They sit at tables having pre-Christmas get-togethers, smiling, laughing, seemingly unaware of what's drawing nearer for them. They're ordering food and wine as if they'll be able to eat and drink until the end of time. Whereas Don is travelling down this road he's been down thousands of times before, and all his comings and goings feel like practice runs for this moment when his fate is about to be revealed, with the street, perhaps, set to disappear.

It has rained all day, unseasonal, tropical rain, and after the storm, scouring sunlight hits the streets. We park on the edge of the city and start walking along the traffic-clogged road towards the oncologist's office.

Earlier, Don had said to me, 'I reckon I'm going to be okay.'

In that moment, I'd pitied him.

The heroes in Grimm's fairytales are often set impossible tasks in order to save themselves or a loved one: a girl must spin straw into gold, another separates lentils from cinders, someone else has to sew six shirts out of nettles and stay silent for as many years; a man must fetch a ring dropped in a red sea, he must eat three hundred oxen leaving not a hair or bone, or find a thousand pearls scattered through the forest. Their odds feel similar to those Don, his very sinew aching, faces.

Trudging up the busy street, I dare to ask, 'Why do you think the results will be good?'

'In the shower this morning, I suddenly felt well. But the feeling is fading now,' he admits, the walking an effort.

I'm trying to prepare us for all outcomes. Information has been meted out so irregularly, it seems we should also be ready to *not* know. 'What if there's no result?'

He presses the crossing button. 'I'll trash the office.'

The air smells of petrol fumes, and office workers, who congregate on the street to smoke, blow out more particulates.

Into the office building and up the tinny lift we go.

It's twelve days until Christmas. Other patients have left partridge- and pear-tree-shaped gifts by the oncologist's reception desk, and I'm suddenly conscious we haven't brought an offering. Traditionally, in epic stories, the lords of death like to be given presents; open to corruption, they appreciate some form of sacrifice. Arriving here empty-handed seems a misstep.

We're ushered into the oncologist's room, and he's wound up by the season. The presents piled on a filing cabinet have given the room a strange party air. The oncologist, a thoughtful man, curious about other people and drawn into their lives beyond the illness, has to remember himself. He's standing in a beautiful linen suit, this refinement providing protection against the chaos of others' blood.

'Has the bone marrow biopsy been performed?' he asks finally.

We say it has and he sits down and starts searching for the outcome in his inbox. 'The results don't seem to have arrived.'

Don and I exchange glances.

The oncologist picks up the phone and makes a call. We can hear the voice of his colleague in the laboratory as he requests the results.

This voice hesitates. In a heart-lurching moment, it's clear something strange has been found. A monster growing in a petri dish.

'Don't tell me, there's AML,' the oncologist groans. He and the other voice discuss a technicality about this other thing.

'No. No, it's *Donald*,' he finally interjects, 'as in Donald Duck.'

And that's it. Someone else, Ron or John or Con—*their* bone marrow has unfortunately developed a new, dire problem. But, we now learn, there's no residual cancer in your father's marrow visible on an analysis of a hundred thousand cells.

Don is still. I am still.

The slow-turning minds of the lottery winners: both of us try to take it in.

There have been people overseas cured of this leukaemia, the oncologist explains. Don is one of these outliers who has had the very rare cancer, and an even rarer recovery. Perhaps if further analysis finds more cancer, he'll need more chemotherapy. But in the meantime, the oncologist doesn't want to press on with the treatment. His advice is to end it now.

A startled smile has spread over Don's face.

The oncologist stands and moves to open the door. He may as well be wearing a pointed hat with sun and moon appliqué, but he's modest about his part in this. Trading in miracles, he can't afford to be astonished. The cauldron has to work again, because on the other side of the door wait a group of people whose own blood could kill them, and he needs us to now leave.

We're standing at the reception desk, paying the bill, and I am laugh-crying when the oncologist comes back out of his room with his phone in his hand. He's just received a text message. His colleague has examined the cells again: this superhuman technology, unimaginable for all but a blip in human history, has shown no detectable cancer on a test of one and a quarter million cells. There is no trace of leukaemia left in Don's blood.

Surrounded by the cellophane-wrapped pot plants, and boxes of chocolates, we're handed this gift. The receptionists allow themselves to show a sweetness they probably can't often express, and direct us quietly to a bar a few streets away where we might enjoy a glass of champagne. In front of the waiting room's strained-looking patients and their supporters, Don is embarrassed as much as stunned by his good fortune.

We walk out into a late-afternoon throng of glaze-eyed, unsteady men and women, who appear to have just left long office Christmas lunches. Store windows are festooned with jewel-tinted tinsel, and shoppers are marching out the doors clasping gilded bags, while Don blinks in this scene, as if unsure of all he's now allowed. We choose a restaurant and sit on the pavement by a street sleek with grease and rain. It's rained so heavily, we later learn, that in some parts of the state cars have floated down the highway. Storm clouds make an early dusk as we ring you boys, at home with the babysitter, and tell you the news. Your excitement, your relief, rushes through the phone, and yes, you too can have a bubbly drink, and yes, even out of champagne flutes.

We let the evening turn around us, with drunk people's high spirits giving way to something darker, and sitting on our charmed patch of footpath, we start to breathe again. Suddenly he and I can look beyond a day, a week. And this is over. This is over. Just like that, we've made it to dry land, and, for now, this is over.

# Fourteen

One day you might come back to this house and find, as adults do, that it seems much smaller. That you are standing before a shrunken white cottage, surprised to find it's only a few paces from the front gate to the veranda. Inside, the rooms' dimensions will be reduced too, and even with an uncanny shaft of light or squeaking floorboard, it might seem incredible that this place was once the locus of all things, that it had the power to draw you in and out each day and remains so fixed in your memory.

Maybe you'll walk down the hall and out through the back door to the garden, which is not in fact a vast parkland with endless places to lose a ball. You'll recall being growled at for some game-winning kick that broke off another plant's new growth, and also moments of truce, working here alongside your father.

Picture this: your father is back in the garden, restored to his home after his long and dangerous wandering.

As he slowly regains energy, he does the tasks he watched build up through his illness. In bursts, he's pruning, and clearing, and replanting.

It is spring once more and, in the news, fires are burning where they shouldn't, authorities are relocating fish from Australia's dying river system, the Reef is turning bone-coloured, and before the year is out the first coughing people will find themselves breathless. Here, though, only the peach tree sends up its pink flares. On the grapevine, crenelated baby leaves burst through with soft white down. The *Sambucus* throws out dark purple feathers, and the *Phlomis*, its silver leaves once used as lamp wicks, has whorl-like, spinebill-attracting flowers.

You two boys are in gumboots, shovelling sand around the garden with half-sized shovels. You're helping Don convert the sandpit you've outgrown into a vegetable patch, and your father now places a seed in each hand of both of you.

The seeds look like shiny white tablets and you push them into the soft earth, up to your first or second finger joints.

'One here, one here, one here,' Don directs.

The sky's full of nothing but blue. All the birds are down around us in this forest he has planted.

'One here … That's too deep.'

A finger worm retracts.

'Good.'

Don's fork turns the soil, making furrows in which to now plant root vegetables. He pulls lumps of potato, all sprouting, out of a brown paper bag. You and your brother examine the purpling flesh, marbled like an old book's endpapers, and plant the lumps in rows. Don then marks each row with a stick.

'People will be talking about these potatoes for centuries to come,' he assures you.

You drift around him, watering, or spreading more sand to other places in the garden. Your father, while he has come back to us, would tell you he's changed after his voyaging in the land of the dead. It's not quite immortality he's been gifted. Every three months he requires a blood test, and his physical recovery is taking time. His brain and limbs have slowly lost their chemical dullness but a metallic taste remains, as if the drugs stay on his tongue. There's also been a psychic adjustment. All the life after his illness seems different, as does all the life before it.

Those days of his youth on the farm, hot days of early summer before school broke up for Christmas, cutting seed potato and dousing it in the deadly, sweet-smelling chemical. Then more days spent standing on the back of the potato planter being towed behind his father's tractor. Never on flat ground, always on a hill. They'd start the lopsided journey in the morning and only finish planting when it grew dark. How *recent* this feels now to your father, the scent of earth and superphosphate, how potent and close, when at the time, it seemed like the stuff before real life started.

Don's here and there—with his sons and in his childhood, love drawing him back and forth. Just as one day you'll be somewhere else and memory will call you here, to these days.

Inside the house, I've started to pack up the board books

I read you and Gabriel as babies. Your reading material is another marker of time passing. I started as your country's librarian. Your tiny fingers learning to negotiate the cardboard-page turns. Our bodies pressed together, the stories' rhythm like a heartbeat. Those early years moved so slowly, and now you're at school, with Gabriel about to follow; time has sped up, and childhood seems a place we reside, as children at least, only briefly. Into the box go a host of talking animals. We need more room on the shelves for chapter books.

These nights, you read to yourself while I read to your brother. You like it if we sit nearby, although it irritates you if, like a bad actor, I give the story too much expression, imposing myself on it. Then you might glance over at the page and pick up a dropped word or the mispronunciation of a siren—'*Nee-Nah!* Not *Nee-Naw!*'

Usually, though, you are in a world of pirates, or multistorey treehouses, or magicians, ensorcelled yourself, statue-still between the page turns. The quickening a story can provoke. It's the dream you can control. You can skim or skip the page that scares you. You can reread it if you like being scared, and no one nearby guesses what's going on. The bedazzlement, the secret drench of it.

'Is it true that *anything is possible?*' you look up from the page to ask.

'No, it's not true.'

Like me, you're conscious of the proximity of the different ending, of a plot change that didn't come, but which also always comes. You know that grief cannot be avoided. And that when it finds a person, they might look the same but they're changed: their missing person has altered the atmosphere in the house, the classroom, the playground; on birthdays and holidays; amongst friends and with the parent who survives.

You've watched your friend make it through the scorched lands of grief and he's been helped on his way by books. There's a long, rich list of works where the loss of a parent is shot through with magic. You've read some of them too and found that unexpected consolations can emerge like green shoots from blackened earth. Not just your friend, but others have survived and found ways to again love life.

When we are young, we are still learning the spells that can be cast by finding the exact name for those things that haunt us. In writing about this episode of our lives, I have the illusion of controlling it: 'there's a cool web of language winds us in', wrote the poet Robert Graves to describe the way adults use words to alleviate pain; 'we have speech, to chill the angry day/And speech, to … spell away the overhanging night.' I can choose which parts of this experience to emphasise, and to hide, to linger over or speed up. The moment we put something that's happened to us into a sentence we put it a degree or two further away, the better to make sense of it. Then, the 'cool web of language' winds us into a silken, sticky net of stories.

'Don't adventures ever have an end?' Bilbo Baggins asks Frodo. 'I suppose not. Someone else always has to carry on the story.' Storytelling's subject and purpose is survival. Someone tells a tale; the tale itself may be all that endures, but it's being passed along, transmitted. And when there's no more forest to get lost and found in, no more animals that turn and whisper some vital clue, the last adult and child will be sitting in the ashes and one will tell the other a tale about ash. We're wired for it, and it keeps us going.

One evening, you present your father with a handwritten list of his complete bedtime stories. He hasn't told you any of them in ages, and you think he should restart the tradition. Gabriel, his calm kindness still regulating the rest of us as he grows older, now listens closely too. Don settles back on the couch. I turn out the light, and his voice begins to flicker in and out of the dark.

Part of me would like Don to tell you both something fitted to the moment, something elegiac. He can make a tale out of anything, so why not take, say, the strawberry tree in our garden. Its timber is hard but doesn't grow straight. In a particular kind of tale, someone wise and old would cut a branch. They'd carve and sand it. They'd sing spells into the wood's grain. Then a bow or staff or wand would be placed in a ready young hand …

But your father has no interest in the upswell of violins, the schmaltz of a luminous stag shooting from a wand. He likes a tale kept plain. Stories about small-scale acts of wonder. Also, he doesn't want you boys always thinking of his departure, and so instead you hear about a spider that has lived comfortably behind a picture frame for many moons, until humans begin spring-cleaning. These finicky people force the spider to seek shelter in increasingly absurd places. You both laugh as it hides behind hair curlers and drying underpants, before scurrying up a chimney to find a crack in the roof's mortar, where, for the first time, it sees a brilliant, star-filled sky ... Every catastrophe brings the chance of a new life.

You may have engineered this performance to keep Don close, to keep an eye on him, but he outlasts you; he often still waits for you both to drift off.

Even going to sleep has the old plotline: separation, adventure, return.

And each morning is a fresh quest. Sunlight finds its way through the gaps in the drawn curtains. The dark and all its frights are gone again, but sometimes you don't want to leave the bed. The impression of your body on the mattress seems a sign that this is your true place. Your father and I nag and cajole you through the mundane steps it takes to get up and leave the house. Your brother still has the luxury of spending part of the week at home, an unfairness that hurts as you and I set off walking up the street towards the school.

On these days, you're the reluctant hero of the story, but there's no choice. Our brains cast us as our tale's central character, *we're all* someone we have to perpetually glimpse in the mirror, and hear speak, and follow around on the journey to find meaning in our lives. At the school gates, you hold the straps of your backpack and trudge to the classroom, a blank stare perfected. The lessons you've recently learned you keep to yourself.

Childhood is an epic. A perilous quest full of strange and beautiful and dangerous possibilities. It's a struggle, not knowing where to place yourself. The desire for autonomy runs headlong into the signs of stress in grown-ups. You don't yet know what your special talent will be, what sword you can pull from a stone. And yet, Don has brought us back intelligence from the land of the dead. In a different, more potent way, we know our time is precious. 'We die. That may be the meaning of life. But we do language. That may be the measure of our lives,' as Toni Morrison wrote.

I write this in the hours you're at school—the opportunistic scribe—not wanting to leave my desk until the last possible moment. Through the wall, I can hear Don writing too, the rhythm of his fingers on the keyboard. When it's my turn to fetch you, I hurry up the road towards the school with a head full of shifting paragraphs, trying not to be late again.

Seeing your face amongst all the other faces is a favourite moment. I scan your expression for how you've fared, the ratio of triumphs to tribulations, and we start to walk back home.

On these afternoons I have to settle myself into your—and, if he's with us, your brother's—sense of time. The length of your steps, the meandering inquisitiveness of your minds, the poking around you still do with sticks to investigate the footpath's hard trash or flowers jutting through fence posts; your indifference to *my* time.

I close my eyes and feel the sun on my face as I walk. I remember to swallow the day's grievances and feel this fortune. And I make these lines from C.P. Cavafy's 'Ithaka' a prayer for you two boys:

*Pray that your journey be long*
*May there be many summer mornings*
*When with pleasure and joy*
*You will come upon harbors seen for the first time.*

See! The poet is alive again … in a way. It's a magic act anyone who reads can perform. Open a book and you bring the writer back to life. It's a trick you've already been doing. By reading a classic you visit the underworld and, becoming acquainted with the dead, download the lessons their work contains, take in their radiance.

We cross the narrow threshold from the gate to the front door, passing the purple leaves of the crab apple, and balancing bags and balls, trail into the still-to-you roomy spaces. Down the hall and through to the kitchen. Look out the back window.

A silver dart shoots through the tangle of creepers on the side fence. The honeyeaters have returned.

One lands in the strawberry tree that contains this year's nest. The tree is covered in white, bell-like flowers and the bird balances on twig headstocks, twisting to drink the nectar. These acrobatics set the bells quivering. The bird flips a flower full circle, tugging on the stamen as if it's a striker, then making the harmonics with its trilling. Blossoms shower down. The bird bath under the tree is overflowing with swollen, water-logged chimes.

If one day either of you boys takes this book off a shelf, the scent of time rising from the binding, close your eyes for me.

Picture the glow of the tree's smooth orange bark, then the black-eyed shimmer of the bird. If the bird disappears into the leaves, know that it's still there. It's still there. As am I. As your father is. Close to you, all together, safe, inside these pages.

# Notes

Page 3, A child's fear of the dark, Freud believed was connected to separation anxiety. In *Introduction to Psychoanalysis* (1917) he wrote, 'I once heard a child who was afraid of the darkness call out: "Auntie, talk to me, I'm frightened." "But what good will that do? You can't see me?" To which the child replied: "If someone talks, it gets lighter."' According to the analyst Margaret Stewart Temeles, a fear of the dark is connected to a 'young child becoming aware of something that he/she cannot fathom'.

Page 3, In the 1920s the developmental psychologist Jean Piaget recorded rituals that children used to make bedtime safe in *The Child's Conception of the World*, translated by Joan and Andrew Tomlinson, Rowman & Littlefield, 2007.

Page 5, After her twin brother, Yama: This myth is recorded in *A Sanskrit Reader: Text and Vocabulary and Notes*, by Charles Rockwell Lanman, Hansebooks, 2019.

Page 16, In European folkstories of the Middle Ages, plague is the constant background: I have quoted from *The Annals of Ireland by Friar John Clyn*, edited by Bernadette Williams, Four Courts Press, 2007. I've taken William Tyndale's 1528 complaint that folk literature could be as 'filthy as herte can think' from Seth Lerer's invaluable *Children's Literature: A Reader's History, from Aesop to Harry*

*Potter*, The University of Chicago Press, 2008; and the information about Cinderella is from Iona and Peter Opies' *The Classic Fairy Tales*, Oxford University Press, 1974. I am also grateful to the work of Kimberley Reynolds—I've quoted from her 2014 article 'Perceptions of Childhood' on the British Library website—and Maurice Saxby. Saxby, a champion of children's literature in Australia, quotes the German schoolmaster of 1787 in *Books in the Life of a Child*, Macmillan, 1997.

Page 17, Young readers, being born of original sin: James Janeway's *A Token for Children, being an Exact Account of the Conversion, Holy and Exemplary Lives, and Joyful Deaths of Several Young Children* (1671) stayed in print for over two hundred years. Janeway had just cause to feel the threat of his own death was ever-present. He preached during the 1665 Great Plague of London; witnessed the 1666 Great Fire of London; survived depression and two assassination attempts, one bullet passing through his hat; and died of tuberculosis aged thirty-eight.

Page 24, Sex was cleared away first: For information on the Grimm brothers I have found the following works useful: *Clever Maids: The Secret History of The Grimm Fairy Tales*, Valerie Paradiž, Basic Books, 2005; *The Brothers Grimm and Their Critics: Folktales and the Quest for Meaning*, Christa Kamenetsky, Ohio University Press, 1992; *The Brothers Grimm*, Ruth Michaelis-Jena, Routledge and Kegan Paul, 1970; *The Brothers Grimm: From Enchanted Forests to the Modern World*, Jack Zipes, St Martin's Press, 2002.

Page 25, What you find really terrifying, though, is 'Sleeping Beauty': Charles Perrault's 1697 version of the tale contains the funniest line of all fairytales: 'The prince, trembling and full of wonder, approached' the somnambulant woman. 'But he was careful not to tell her that she was dressed like his grandmother.' (Quoted in *Once Upon A Time: On the Nature of Fairy Tales*, Max Luthi, translated by Chadeayne and Gottwald, Indiana University Press, 1976.) Also, was Emily Dickinson thinking of the bad fairy and her coma curse when she wrote of 'A long, long sleep, a famous sleep/ That makes no show for dawn'?

Page 25, Is it the dark or sleep itself: C.S. Lewis described his childhood nightmares as 'a window opening on what is hardly less than Hell'. (*Surprised by Joy: The Shape of My Early Life*, Fount Paperbacks, 1977.) E. Nesbit wrote: 'For a child who is frightened, the darkness and the silence of its lonely room are only a shade less terrible than the wild horrors of dreamland. One used to lie awake in the silence, listening, listening to the pad-pad of one's heart, straining one's ears to make sure that it was not the pad-pad of something else, something quite unspeakable creeping towards one out of the horrible, dense dark. One used to lie quite, quite still, I remember, listening, listening.' (*Long Ago When I Was Young*, E. Nesbit, Ronald Whiting & Wheaton, 1966.)

Page 26, The American poet Robert Penn Warren was also an older father and I quote from his poem '3. Lullaby: Moonlight Lingers' from *The Collected Poems of Robert Penn Warren*, edited by John Burt, Louisiana State University Press, 1998.

Page 28, Flinders, I read later: His story is told in *The Life of Matthew Flinders*, Miriam Estensen, Allen & Unwin, 2002.

Page 29, 'Augustus Earle,' Don continues: In 1824, eight years before he voyaged with Darwin, the thirty-year-old Earle was abandoned on a remote island, an experience he detailed in *Narrative of a Residence in New Zealand and Journal of a Residence in Tristan da Cunha*, Augustus Earle, Oxford at the Clarendon Press, 1966. Earle's watercolour, *Solitude, Watching the Horizon at Sun Set, in the Hopes of Seeing a Vessel*, depicting himself on a cliff, is in the National Library of Australia.

Page 38, On one of my research binges I found 'Sources of Children's Knowledge about Death and Dying', by Sarah Longbottom and Virginia Slaughter, which appeared in *Philosophical Transactions of the Royal Society*, B Volume 373, Issue 1754.

Page 40, When did our children's bookshelves come: In *Inventing Wonderland: The Lives of Lewis Carroll, Edward Lear, J.M. Barrie, Kenneth Grahame and A.A. Milne*, Methuen, 2001, Jackie Wullschläger describes the Edwardian obsession with childhood.

In the shadow of World War I, Barrie cut the line, 'To die would be an awfully big adventure,' from *Peter Pan*, as is detailed by Lesley Clement in her introduction to *Global Perspectives on Death in Children's Literature*, edited by Lesley Clement and Leyli Jamali, Routledge, 2015. After Barrie's adopted son was killed on a French battlefield, the cultural valorisation of death struck him as grotesque. Paul Fussell, in

*The Great War and Modern Memory*, Oxford Univeristy Press, 1975, writes of the euphemistic language used after the war.

For a glimpse at the real age of some of our best-known children's stories, I recommend Ferris Jabr's 'The Story of Storytelling', *Harpers*, March, 2019. Jabr writes of the anthropologist Jamie Tehrani's use of phylogentics, a family tree of story derivations, to date tales like 'Beauty and the Beast' and 'Rumpelstiltskin' back to more than two and a half thousand years ago.

**Page 41, Death entered the medical miracle of the twentieth century:** Regarding our changing attitudes to death, the French historian Philippe Ariès wrote that for generations death was 'a public ceremony', with family and neighbours gathered in 'the dying man's bedchamber'; and 'until the eighteenth century no portrayal of a deathbed scene failed to include children'. Traditional mourning rituals also involved even the youngest. '[D]eath was both familiar and near, evoking no great fear or awe', which 'offers too marked a contrast' to our attitude, 'where death is so frightful that we dare not utter its name'.

**Page 43, In children's literature, people just accept they're living in a different dimension:** As the German scholar of fairytales Max Lüthi noted in *The European Folktale: Form and Nature*, translated by John Q. Niles, Indiana University Press, 1982, 'The folktale hero who meets with speaking animals, winds, or stars evinces neither astonishment nor fear.' And that's because these tales suggest that 'side by side with the ordinary world exists the otherworld'. In this place, the hero 'lacks all sense of the extraordinary'.

Page 46, 'I observe the *Phisician*,' wrote John Donne:  Meditation VI from *The Complete Poetry and Selected Prose of John Donne*, edited by Charles M. Coffin (!), Modern Library, 1952.

Page 58, The first literary orphan many children meet: Carle's quote about the helpless egg comes from an interview in *The Guardian*, May 2016.

Page 61, I shift from researching children's literature to those who wrote it: For my series of biographical sketches I'm grateful to have read the Grimm biographies listed above, as well as *Hans Christian Andersen: The Life of a Storyteller*, Jackie Wullcshläger, Allen Lane, 2000; *Hans Christian Andersen: The Story of his Life and Work 1805–75*, Elias Bredsdorff, C. Scribner's Sons, 1983; *The One I Knew the Best of All*, Frances Hodgson Burnett, Frederick Warne & Co. Ltd, 1974; *Frances Hodgson Burnett*, Phyllis Bixler, Twayne, Boston, 1984; *The Extraordinary Life of E. Nesbit*, Elisabeth Galvin, Pen & Sword History, 2018; *Kenneth Grahame: An Innocent in the Wild Wood*, Alison Prince, Allison & Busby, 1994; *Inventing Wonderland: The Lives of Lewis Carroll, Edward Lear, J.M. Barrie, Kenneth Grahame and A.A. Milne*, Jackie Wullschläger, Methuen, 2001; *Mary Poppins She Wrote: The Life of P.L. Travers*, Valerie Lawson, Simon & Schuster, 2013; *Selected Journals of L.M. Montgomery*, edited by Mary Rubio and Elizabeth Waterston, Oxford University Press, 2014; *J.R.R. Tolkien: A Biography*, Humphrey Carpenter, George Allen & Unwin, 1977; *Surprised by Joy: The Shape of My Early Life*, C.S. Lewis, Fount Paperbacks, 1977; *The Narnian: The*

*Life and Imagination of C.S. Lewis*, Alan Jacobs, Harper Collins, 2005; *Saint-Exupéry: A Biography*, Stacy Schiff, Henry Holt, 2006; *Boy: Tales of Childhood*, Roald Dahl, Penguin, 2011; *Storyteller: The Life of Roald Dahl*, Donald Sturrock, Harper Press, 2010. However, I acknowledge that C.S. Lewis thoroughly distained the 'type of critic who speculates about the genesis of your book [like] the amateur psychologist … He knows what unacknowledged wishes you were gratifying … By definition you are unconscious of the things he professes to discover. Therefore, the more loudly you disclaim them, the more right he must be, [but] They have not had their author on the sofa, nor heard his dreams, and had the whole case history.'

**Page 71, It's important, I've read, for the sick parent:** Before discussing the cancer with our children, we read *Talking to Kids About Cancer: A Guide for People with Cancer, their Families and Friends*, Cancer Council Australia, 2018 (available online); *How to Help Children Through a Parent's Serious Illness*, Kathleen McCue, St Martin's, 2011.

**Page 75, The forest is where the protagonist finds they've ventured too far:** Francis Spufford, in his wonderful *The Child That Books Built*, suggests: 'If the forest is where we go when, in Bruno Bettelheim's words, we "lose the framework which gave structure to our past life", we can go there at any age. Any time can be the time when structure collapses and the tangle of roots and branches surrounds us. The order we are living by ends without warning or after long struggle … And for the third or fifth or umpteenth time the leaves are under our feet again.'

Page 80, But your father has loved the bush: I have quoted liberally from *The Bush*, Don Watson, Penguin, 2014, throughout this book.

Page 92, The boiling, creaming, thundering sea: This description is from Richmond Lattimore's *The Odyssey of Homer: A Modern Translation*, Harper & Row, 1967. I have also quoted from the children's version *The Adventures of Odysseus*, Lupton et al., Barefoot Books, 2015, and also the translation by A.T. Murray, Harvard University Press, 1919 (online version at the Perseus Digital Library).

Page 97, Descent narratives involve someone visiting an underworld: *Mythology: The Voyage of the Hero*, David Adams Leeming, J.B. Lippincott, 1973, details tales of the underworld in different cultures.

Page 116, Criss-crossing all of Australia are sacred stories of the seven sisters: I'm grateful to have read *Songlines: Tracking the Seven Sisters*, edited by Margot Neale, National Museum of Australia Press, 2018.

Page 118, Aboriginal Australians had been singing about the sisters for thousands of years before Homer: This reference to the Pleiades comes from 'Astronomy and Constellations in the Iliad and Odyssey', by E. Theodossiou and V.N. Maniamanis, *The Journal of Astronomical History and Heritage*, 14(1), 2011.

Page 124, When he started school, this boy was already reading chapter books: John Steinbeck's recollection of learning to read is quoted in John Morgensten's *Playing With Books: A Study of the*

*Reader as Child*, McFarland & Company Inc., 2009; Beverly Cleary recalls her struggles in *A Girl from Yamhill*, HarperCollins, 2016; Toni Morrison made these remarks in a speech on 14 August 2016 as the 57th Edward MacDowell Medalist; Graham Greene's memory is from his book *The Lost Childhood*, Eyre & Spottiswoode, 1951.

Page 126, On a quest, the hero's most terrifying confrontation: Frederick Turner, in *Epic*, writes: 'Despite Tolkien's spirited defence of epic monsters they are still regarded, I believe, with embarrassment and even scorn' as 'camp' or 'juvenile' or 'representing some kind of code for hegemonic marginalisation of the Other. Yet we have all dreamed of monsters.' Turner suggests monsters are 'a challenge to the normal process by which we perceptually and cognitively identify something. A monster is in itself a statement that our world has limits,' and past these limits are things we do not understand and may not be able to control. It is Turner's point that the most frightening form of the monster is 'the monster within'. Certainly, Harry Potter discovers he has part of evil Lord Voldemort's soul embedded within him: 'You were the seventh Horcrux, Harry. The Horcrux he never meant to make.' And Ged, in Ursula K. Le Guin's *A Wizard of Earthsea*, finds himself being chased by a creature 'without lips or ears or eyes' that 'shrank and blackened, crawling on four short taloned legs': this 'foul, cruel thing', he realises, is his own shadow.

Page 130, Patrick Ness's breathtaking *A Monster Calls* (2011) was conceived by Siobhan Dowd, before she died herself of breast cancer.

Dowd wanted healing to be the work's theme. 'It is really my paeon to the great, ancient tree, the yew,' she claimed, 'as all the Taxol drugs that so successfully treat breast cancers are derived from it'.

Page 126, The reality of this switches on: Regarding a fear of spiders, C.S. Lewis believed they could terrify because 'Their angular limbs, their jerky movements, their dry, metallic noises, all suggest either machines that have come to life or life degenerating into mechanism.'

Page 133, The Brothers Grimm believed that the poetic 'animation of all nature': Wilhelm Grimm, in particular, took delight in documenting language—from children's games to old superstitions and expressions—which gave nature a poetic life force. (For instance, the German saying 'Now God shuts the door to Heaven' was meant to encourage little children into bed. Stars were 'the golden nails on the heavenly gate'; the moon, 'the lock'. Twinkling stars were a sign that children should rush to bed before the gate slammed shut.) At heart, fairy stories express 'the desire of men to hold communion with all living things', wrote Tolkien.

Page 141, Much children's literature revolves around the awfulness of adults: In his own advanced years, Maurice Sendak recognised that he had become a grotesque figure to children, and stopped autographing books and going into classrooms. He registered 'the look of alarm and the tears, and they stare at me [with] pure hatred. Who is this elderly, short man sitting behind a desk who's going to take their book away ... to write something in it ... It's horrible for them. And I become horrible unwittingly. I make children cry.' This Sendak quote, along with that used in this book regarding his sense of boyhood, is taken from an interview with Terry Gross replayed on National Public Radio, 8 May 2012.

Page 145, Poowong, the name of the town where he went to primary school, was listed as meaning carrion in Daniel Bunce's *Language of the Aborigines of the Colony of Victoria and other Australian Districts*, Slater, Williams & Hodgson, 1851.

Page 146, The idea of language being an animated, animating force was written about by the anthropologist Bronisław Malinowski in *Coral Gardens and Their Magic* of 1935: 'this knowledge of the right words, appropriate phrases … gives man a power over and above his own limited field of personal action'.

Page 157, 'may my heart always be open to little birds': from the e.e. cummings poem of the same title, in *Complete Poems 1904–1962*, Liveright, 1994.

Page 159, For Louisa May Alcott, wilderness provided respite from bitter poverty: This is detailed in *Eden's Outcasts: The Story of Louisa May Alcott and Her Father*, John Matteson, W.W. Norton, 2007; and *Louisa May Alcott: The Woman Behind Little Women*, Harriet Reisen, Picador, 2010. I have drawn from the biographies listed earlier on other children's writers' connection to nature.

Page 160, In this milieu, nature gave Alcott an experience: John Passmore on the shortcoming of the Romantic tradition's positioning of God in nature is quoted in *Ethics in British Children's Literature: Unexamined Life*, Lisa Sainsbury, Bloomsbury, 2015.

Page 165, In most of your books, a creature is used as a cuddly proxy: Lisa Rowe Fraustino points this out in 'The Rights and Wrongs of Anthropomorphism in Picture Books', in *Ethics and Children's Literature*, edited by Claudia Mills, Ashgate, 2014. Rowe Fraustino writes: 'Judging from animal fantasy, one would never know that a rabbit mother in the wild may produce seven or eight litters per season, of four to twelve babies each. She visits them to nurse a few times a day and otherwise stays away from the kits keeping watch from a safe distance lest her strong scent draw predators to the nest.' The mother 'won't chase them down and drag them home', as the mother rabbit does in Margaret Wise Brown's classic *Runaway Bunny*.

*The Rabbits*, John Marsden and Shaun Tan, Hachette Australia, 2020, tells an allegorical story of colonisation through the invasion of rabbits. Tan's surreal, revolutionary *Tales from The Inner City* also envisions an alternate world taken over by animals.

Page 178, Soon after Don's diagnosis, I read an essay by the children's literature historian, Francelia Butler: It was 'Death in Children's Literature', *Children's Literature*, Johns Hopkins University Press, Volume 1, 1972. Butler refers to the *Motif-Index of Folk-Literature*, by American Folklorist Stith Thompson, often called *Thompson's Motif-Index*.

Page 185, One night, you produce a reader titled *In Search of the Mummy*: This was written by Meredith Costain, ETA/Cuisenaire, 2001.

Page 227, *Pray that your journey be long*: Cavafy's 'Ithaka' is quoted in *Innocence and Experience*, edited by Harrison and Maguire, Lothrop, Lee and Shepard, 1987.

Page 227, It's a magic act anyone who reads can perform: I've drawn on Frederick Turner's point in *Epic* that 'the very possibility that we can talk with the dead immediately changes time from a meaning-less succession of events to a multidimensional manifold'. The hero returns from the underworld with information which is of 'practical use, both tactical and strategic' and 'a call to action, an assignment of a task or duty'.

Page 227, One lands in the strawberry tree: Hieronymus Bosch painted the strawberry tree in *The Garden of Earthly Delights*. (The nudes are lounging underneath enjoying the fruit.) Pliny the Elder believed this tree's fruit gave honey a desirable bitterness. Ovid also writes of it in 'The Golden Age' of *Metamorphoses,* and it's in Virgil's *Aeneid*. In other words, a character from various epics has been grow-ing in our garden.

# Acknowledgements

My great thanks to Bernard Caleo, Anna Goldsworthy, Judith Thurman, Jaye Kranz, Andrew Wylie, Tracy Bohan, Ben Ball, Meredith Rose, Anna Walker, Allison Colpoys, Anna O'Grady, Michelle Swainson, Constantine Tam, Priscilla Blake, Jovelyn Barrion, Eddel Gauten, Ellie Watson and Juliana and Toby Hooper.